HOW TO BECOME A

MARKETING SUPERSTAR

HOW TO BECOME A

MARKETING SUPERSTAR

Unexpected Rules
That Ring
the Cash Register

JEFFREY J. FOX

New York

Library of Congress Cataloging-in-Publication Data

Fox, Jeffrey J.
    How to become a marketing superstar : unexpected rules that ring the cash register / Jeffrey J. Fox.
        p. cm.
    ISBN 0-7868-6824-4
    1. Marketing. I. Title.

HF5415 .F663 2003
380.1—dc21

                                2002038889

Hyperion books are available for special promotions and premiums. For details contact Hyperion Special Markets, 77 West 66th Street, 11th floor, New York, New York 10023-6298, or call 212-456-0133.

FIRST EDITION

10 9 8 7 6 5 4 3 2 1

With inspiration from the 1959 hit song by

the wonderful Shirelles . . .

This is dedicated to the ones I love.

Each night before I go to bed my babies,

I whisper a little prayer for you my babies,

and tell the stars above.

This is dedicated to the ones I love.

Acknowledgments

Mary Ellen O'Neill, senior editor, Hyperion (New York). Whose supply of colored pencils is endless, one of which she uses to draw the line between the witty and the wacky.

Doris Michaels, Doris Michaels Literary Agency (New York). Whose unflagging enthusiasm has made the Fox series of books available to readers in every language in every great country on the planet.

All contributors at Fox & Company, Fox Family, Hyperion, and the Doris S. Michaels Literary Agency.

Contents

CONTENTS

CONTENTS

CONTENTS

CONTENTS

CONTENTS

CONTENTS

CONTENTS

Because it is its purpose to create a customer, any business enterprise has two—and only these two—basic functions: marketing and innovation. Marketing is the distinguishing, the unique function of a business.

—Peter Drucker, Clark Professor of Social Science and Management, Claremont & Graduate University (ret.)

All industry begins with the customer and his or her needs, not with a patent, a raw material, or a selling skill.

—Ted Leavitt, professor emeritus, Harvard Business School

INTRODUCTION

This book is for any enterprise that invests time or treasure to get and keep customers.

There is an old advertising industry line that says "50 percent of advertising is wasted, but no one knows which 50 percent." This is not a joke, nor is it true. It is a feint, a finesse by the advertising industry to deflect examination or measurement of how much communication money is squandered. Any serious, objective review of ads, in all media, shows that *at least* 90 of every 100 ads are not read or are unintelligible or are superficial or don't promote the brand. Money is squandered because of weak messages, cluttered images, improper media usage, and poor creative strategy.

Advertising is not the only gaping hole in the marketer's

purse. The cost of poor personal selling is also a huge money waster. It is estimated that 95 percent of all salespeople never ask for the order. So few salespeople pre-plan a sales call that selling is one of the least efficient and least effective parts of the marketing mix. The ineptitude of personal selling is masked by the reality that 25 percent of all sales are unilaterally made by the customer. The customer studies the product, decides for herself, and buys without, or despite, a salesperson.

This reality is why, in boom times, certain salespeople and selling organizations, as well as certain advertisers and their ad agencies, consider themselves geniuses, yet in down times poor sales performance is always the fault of others or of weak markets.

It is easy to become a salesperson. It is easy to call oneself a marketer. The barriers to enter those jobs, particularly sales, are low. But to become a sales rainmaker, or to become a marketing superstar, is immensely challenging.

Marketing superstars make the cash register ring, ring, *ka-ching, ka-ching*. If you need to be, want to be, or are a marketing superstar, this book is for you.

• I •

Ka-ching! Ka-ching!
Marketer's Music

Ka-ching! *Ka-ching!* The worldwide sound of a cash register ringing. The sound of a sale. Literal music to the merchant, symbolic music to the marketing superstar. *Ka-ching* when the slot machine pays off. *Ka-ching* when the ice cream man makes change. *Ka-ching* when check-writing software pays a bill.

Ka-ching is a synonym for generating revenue. It's the sound the rainmaker hears when a deal is struck. *Ka-ching* is what the marketer hopes for when placing an ad. *Ka-ching* is what the retailer, the movie maker, the concert promoter hears above the din of the crowd rushing in.

Ka-ching is what the manufacturer hears every time the press stamps out a part. *Ka-ching* is what the distributor hears every time a box hits a truck shelf. *Ka-ching* is what the car wash owner hears when it snows, when pollen fills the air, when bugs are flying, and when birds are doo-doo doing.

It is the marketer's job to generate revenue, to ring the cash register. Many people know the words of the *ka-ching* marketing song, but not the tune.

Many people know they have to innovate constantly, but they don't do anything new. Many people know that advertising is *supposed* to sell products, but they run ads that don't connect, don't work, and don't sell a thing. Many people know that salespeople must plan every sales call, but they don't train their sales staff. Such people know the words of the marketing song but not the tune.

Marketing superstars know the words and sing and dance to the tune . . .

> ♪ It don't mean a thing, ♪
> If it don't go *ka-ching* . . .
> ♪ Doo-bop. Doo-bop. Doo-bop. ♪

· II ·

Deeply Understand the Definition of Marketing

*T*he long definition of marketing is the profitable identification, attraction, getting, and keeping of good
("okay") customers. The short definition is the profitable getting and keeping of good customers.

Identification, attraction, and getting are pre-sale functions. Keeping includes all post-sale functions. Market
research, for example, is an Identification activity. Advertising, packaging, and clean stores are Attraction activities. Personal selling, distribution, pricing, product quality, and
smiling clerks are Getting activities. Post-sale activities, such
as delivery, billing, bill collection, customer service, warranty repair, and thank-you notes are Keeping activities.

The only sustaining life force in any organization, in any

enterprise, is the getting and keeping of customers (sometimes called members, patients, students, parishioners). Every single job in a company must directly or indirectly help to get and keep customers. Everybody should always be thinking how to help get and keep customers. This includes people greeters, credit checkers, debt collectors, truck loaders, phone answerers, product makers, and presidents. Every employee's job function is a part of the marketing definition.

Marketing is the epicenter of the organization. Marketing is more than the sales force, more than advertising, pricing, packaging, promotion, and trade shows. Marketing is responsible for creating products that fill customer needs, for quality control, and for accounts receivable, inventories, and collections.

Thus, all company departments and functions must be headed by people with a strong customer-first marketing attitude. The manufacturing manager who never meets customers is not customer aware. The R&D scientist who never meets a customer stays ignorant. The credit manager who sees collections as a battle, and not a customer-keeping opportunity, is anti-marketing. The president who does not spend 40–60 percent of his time reading about, talking to, writing to, or visiting customers is sailing the ship at night without lights or charts.

Every job exists to directly or indirectly get and keep good customers, today and tomorrow. Every person must know how his or her job gets and keeps customers. Every person must do something every day—must work all day—to get and keep customers. (Jobs that don't get and keep customers are temporary, unnecessary, or should be outsourced.) Employees must be directed and trained as to why their jobs are important, and how to do them well.

The definition of marketing is simple. The doing of marketing is hard.

• III •

The Superstar
Marketing Company

Great companies don't talk about marketing, they execute marketing. In too many companies, the phrase "close to customer" is 95 percent of the conversation yet 5 percent of the action. In true marketing companies, the CEO and all the top people spend lots of time with customers listening and selling. Spending time with customers is a hundred times more important than attending staff meetings and reading monthly reports. Companies do what the top guys do, and in marketing companies the top guys sell, sell, sell. Many of the best salespeople in the world are not found in big corporate sales forces. They are found running small businesses, where they are the top guys. In superstar marketing companies a person's attitude toward customers is carefully considered in the hiring process. All employees are expected and trained to appreciate the good customer. The person who double-checks the spelling of a customer's name is a marketing person. The salesclerk who stays open past closing to serve a late-arriving customer is a marketing person. The company parking lot attendant who greets the visitor with, "Welcome to our company. We're glad you're here," is a marketing person.

Marketing companies want to hire only those people who truly value the customer, who can get the cash register to ring. Consequently, they invest in constant training, which reaches into every aspect of their enterprise, no matter how small. The result is having people in the company willing and able to do things that employees in other companies won't, don't, can't, or aren't allowed to do.

Can you imagine any employee at Disney World too important to pick up a discarded soda cup? Can you visualize a salesperson at L.L.Bean quibbling with a customer over returned merchandise? Can you believe that Al Pacino or Meryl Streep would ever walk off a stage because the lighting, or anything, was wrong? Of course not!

In great marketing companies everyone has the authority and the duty to use their best judgment to do what is necessary to take care of the customer. At Kodak, the production people have total control over product quality. At Toyota, assembly-line workers can bring the production line to a halt to fix a quality problem. In the Ritz-Carlton hotel chain every employee who is alerted to a customer problem owns that problem until the customer is satisfied. And every Ritz-Carlton employee can spend up to $2,000, without authorization, to make customer problems go away.

A marketing company knows the total dollar value of a customer. They put a time value on the customer relationship. For example, if a woman (or man) spends $45 every three weeks at a beauty salon, and if well treated and well satisfied can be expected to remain a customer for three years, the salon owner values that woman at $2,340 (52 visits over 3 years at $45 per visit). The salon owner values her customer at $2,340 every single time she sees the customer. This is why the smart grocer, car dealer, airline, machine tool builder, stockbroker, and steelmaker cheerfully, enthusiastically pay heed to their customers. The foolish car dealer and the careless kitchen cabinet maker see the sale as the end of the relationship with the customer. And then it is.

Successful marketing companies look at every investment decision with the same simple analysis: "Will this investment help us sell more?" If the investment improves quality, lowers cost without hurting quality, improves selling skills, increases brand awareness, creates new products, or in any way betters the offering to a customer, they will do it.

Superstar marketing companies pursue market share gains

relentlessly and continuously. But they know that market share is a function of pervasive and persuasive marketing. Market share is a scoreboard entry.

At superstar marketing companies, marketing is manifest. That's why they win.

• IV •

"This Is Customer Money!"

*E*very paycheck, for every employee, from the busboy to the chef, from the picker to the packer, from the trainee to the CEO, must literally or figuratively be stamped: THIS IS CUSTOMER MONEY! This will remind everyone in the organization for whom they work.

XYZ Corporation
Payroll Services

THIS IS
CUSTOMER
MONEY!

PAY to the order of: Jane Workmanship $1,000.00

In the amount of: One Thousand and No Dollars

ABC National Bank
XXXX XXXX XXXXX XXXXXX XXXX XXXXXXXXX

John Q. Treasurer

In an established business, the paychecks are funded by the customer. (In a start-up, or a turnaround, the paychecks may be funded by investors or lenders. But the investors and lenders expect to get paid back, and the payback will ultimately come from customers.) The money that covers the paychecks does not come from the owner or the boss. The money does not come from a distant bank account or a check-paying service or a union. Paychecks come from the customer. Government workers are all paid by their customers, the taxpayers. College professors are paid by the people who pay tuitions, pay taxes, or make donations.

Everybody is paid by the customer. Pay raises, bonuses, job promotions, and worker benefits are paid by the customer.

Marketing superstars and great marketing companies never forget—not for an instant—that their existence depends on the customer.

Customers
Fire Employees Every Day

*E*veryone in every organization works for the customer. Everyone works to make customers happy with the value they receive for their money. To a customer, good value is based on product quality, timely delivery, hassle-free exchange, fresh fruit in the room, an extra ear of corn with a dozen, a sincere smile, a sincere thank-you, or being kept informed on the status of an order, a lawsuit, or a research project. Customers reward the good work of employees by buying more product or services, or telling others good things about the employee's company. When the customers buy the products, that money is used to fund the employees' paychecks and vacations and coffee breaks.

If customers decide they are not getting appropriate value

for their money, and they take their money elsewhere, the selling company has less money to pay its employees, or to pay for anything else. If the company loses revenue, it will be forced to reduce costs to remain viable. If an employee, or group of employees, is not generating an economic return greater than its cost to the company, that cost will be cut and the employee(s) will be terminated. That termination is a direct result of lost customers.

Customers fire employees every day for many reasons. The customer ignored or treated rudely walks out of the store, the restaurant, the dry cleaner. The customer confused by jargon or put off by selling pressure leaves the showroom, the appliance center, the dealership. The customer whose order is not delivered as promised rejects the delivery or purchases from a different source the next time. The customer who hasn't the time or patience to navigate a bewildering electronic phone system hangs up. The customer whose reservation is lost, whose product is damaged, whose account is misbilled, whose flowers don't bloom is a customer at risk.

Recently a major retail chain went out of business, leaving thousands of people jobless. The chain went out of business for various reasons, including incompetent management, ineffectual strategy, poor employee training, and because the customers shunned the stores and the store personnel. A visit to one store in the imperiled chain showed why. A customer planning to buy one hundred appliances (for a new homes subdivision) made an appointment with the store manager to visit the store a half hour earlier than the regular opening time. Arriving exactly thirty minutes before opening, the customer found locked doors. The store manager was MIA (missing in action). Peering through the glass, the customer spotted two employees chatting and drinking coffee. Pinging the window glass with a key caught the attention of the two employees. One of the employees pointedly indicated his watch and mouthed an exaggerated "We're closed!" The other employee held up ten fingers, helpfully instructing the ready, willing, and able-to-buy customer that the store opened at 10:00. Pleased with their educational efforts, the two employees ambled out of sight.

The customer took his business to a company grateful for the orders. The customer fired those two employees, their MIA store manager, and their associates that day.

Months later, the two coffee drinkers, and 19,998 fellow workers, had no customers, no stores, and no paychecks.

· VI ·

Segment Your Customers:
Okay, Not Okay

S mart marketing starts with smart segmentation. Knowledge of your market shapes your product positioning, branding, communication claims, sales approaches, channels, pricing, and packaging. Necessary knowledge of your target segment includes size of market, growth rate of market, demographics, customer needs, competitive offerings, purchase attitudes, and mind-sets.

There are endless ways to segment markets. Some segmentation approaches are more relevant for one marketing company than another, but there is one segmentation scheme that is helpful to all marketers, from the one-person firm to the multinational company.

All markets segment into four types of customers:

- Sophisticated/Okay
- Unsophisticated/Okay
- Sophisticated/Not okay
- Unsophisticated/Not okay

Sophistication is based on the customer's level of experience buying and using your type of product or service. Generally, the more experienced, the more sophisticated.

It is the marketer's job to categorize every customer and every prospect as sophisticated or unsophisticated. The categorization is typically done after a needs-analysis of the customer. A sophisticated buyer or company is not better managed than an unsophisticated company. Some companies invest in sophistication; others deliberately do not. Some companies are sophisticated buying one product and unsophisticated buying others. You may not always be right, and the customer may change its sophistication level, but into one or the other of these two categories the customer must go.

The marketer must create its own definition of "Okay" and "Not okay." For example, "Okay" might mean the customer is local, pays its bills, values technical service, has good managers, is growing. "Not okay" might mean the customer is rude, can't make a decision, is too expensive to serve, haggles over every invoice, is privately held (or publicly owned). Each customer and prospect must be labeled "Okay" or "Not okay."

1. Sophisticated/Okay customers are usually bigger companies. They know what you sell and how to negotiate. Your margins on sales are lower, but the size of the sales are often large.

2. Unsophisticated/Okay customers generate lower revenues but higher margins. These customers rely on the seller for advice, tech service, and other support, and are willing to pay for it.

3. Sophisticated/Not okay customers represent a risk for the marketer. If you decide to sell to this customer, be prepared for low margins, an arduous decision-making process, delays in getting paid, and employee burnout.

4. Unsophisticated/Not okay customers or prospects are to be avoided. This customer does not appreciate your product, does not respect you, is not loyal, and can be costly. Legal fees are not unusual.

Once you have segmented your customers and prospects, you can build a plan on how to sell to them, how to service, how to set billing terms, how to allocate people. Forewarned is forearmed. This segmentation system forewarns you and directs you properly.

Love those "Okay" customers.

· VII ·

The Customer Is Not Always Right

The oldest marketing cliché is "The customer is always right." The cliché is wrong. The right customer is always right. The wrong customer, the "Not okay" customer, is not right for the selling company. Every organization must have its own definition of a good customer, an "Okay" customer. And every organization must have its own definition of a wrong customer, a "Not okay" customer.

"Okay" definitions will vary according to many circumstances, but minimally the good customer should be profitable to the selling company, pay its bills, and pay for what it buys. Good customers are loyal. Good customers spread positive word of mouth and give positive referrals. Good customers can be tough, exacting, impatient, challenging, fickle, finicky, exasperating, demanding, needy, insistent, and a million other things. None of their traits matter if they are a good, "Okay" customer. "Okay" customers are worth the trouble. Deal with them.

A customer can be a wrong customer, a "Not okay" customer, for various reasons. Typically the wrong customer is unprofitable to the selling company. The wrong customer is not worth the price they are paying, the cost to service, the stress caused, or the opportunities they cause the marketer to forgo.

The customer is not always right. Blind acceptance of this cliché can lead to disaster. The wrong customer is always wrong. The "Okay" customer is the right customer. The right customer is king. Genuflect to the king.

• VIII •

Use the Seven Growth Levers

*T*here are seven levers that grow the top line, that grow revenues, that go *ka-ching*. The marketing superstar first isolates each lever and then develops relevant action plans to maximize that growth lever. Here are the seven levers that grow revenues:

1. Introduce new products and innovate.
2. Add new end-user customers in current markets, in new markets, and in new geographies.
3. Sell new applications of existing products to current customers.
4. Reduce customer attrition.

5. Raise prices.
6. Light candles and pray that market demand rises.
7. Acquire companies.

The super marketer has seven files or seven notebooks or seven sheets of paper or seven delegates each dedicated to one growth lever. Each notebook is crammed with ideas, plans, strategies, innovations . . . anything that might possibly ring the cash register. For example, the super marketer's "Reduce Customer Attrition" notebook would include these kinds of notes:

- Identify rate of customer loss.
- Where are we losing customers?
- Do market research among lost customers to find out why they are leaving.
- Reduce warranty claims.
- Add customer service people.
- Step up sales calls.
- Change and increase advertising.
- Exceed competitors' offerings.
- Send thank-you notes to all existing clients.

The marketing superstar's notebook on "Introduce New Products and Innovate" would be organized into categories such as:

- Totally new product categories.
- Line extensions of existing products.
- Updated and new packaging.
- Seasonal products (e.g., Hershey's Halloween candy)
- Repositioning old formulas, old technology, old products as new products (e.g., Ford Motor's 2002 revival of a retro Thunderbird).

Know the growth levers. Have a "Growth Notebook." Fill the notebook with potential ideas to grow your brand or company. Test the ideas, then execute the ideas.

IX

You Must Love
Your Brand

*T*he marketing superstar is the custodian of the brand. You are the custodian of the brand's image, equity, promise, and future. You must believe in what your brand means to its customers. You must understand and appreciate your brand's legacy. You must be passionate about your brand. You must be publicly and privately proud to sell your brand. You must protect your brand from misuse or misapplication by others in the organization.

Your brand could be a product, a family of products, your company, or a combination. Whatever your brand represents, you must love the brand!

You must love the brand and live the brand. The blood of the brand must flow through your veins. There is a difference between loving a brand and managing a brand. Loving a brand means living the brand, making the brand a part of you. Loving and living the brand leads to long-lasting success. Managing a brand is minding, administering, and maintaining, which leads to mediocrity.

You must understand the value delivered by your brand so well that you are never shy about its price. You must be able to articulate the quantified, dollarized value of every benefit and every point of difference of your brand.

Not all brands are for everybody. There are people who would not do well if their brand were Virginia Slims; others would flourish. There are some who could not be a U.S. Marine; others tattoo "semper fi" high on a hip.

The life and times of the Snapple brand (juice beverages) is an example of the difference between loving a brand and just managing a brand. Snapple was born in Queens, New York. The marketing of the brand was a cocktail of fun, quirky labels, offbeat flavors, and friendly, down-to-earth spokespeople. The entrepreneurs who built the brand were instinctive, savvy marketers. With neither the marketing support money nor sufficient unit volume movement to initially get supermarket distribution, Snapple was sold out of cold boxes in convenience stores, delis, and gas stations. It was pick-and-shovel work to achieve national distribution, but Snapple built a national brand and a national franchise.

Snapple's nontraditional, "amateurish," not-by-the-book marketing created a great brand with a cult-like following.

The original owners sold the Snapple brand to Quaker Oats, a huge consumer products marketing company. Quaker's marketing people must have felt the original brand owner's marketing strategy was hokey, clownish, and unprofessional, for they immediately began to neutralize Snapple's marketing. Quaker's marketing people must have snickered and sneered at Snapple's advertising, for they dropped the Snapple Lady, a spokesperson beloved by the brand customers. Quaker ran professional, expensive television commercials, totally unlike Snapple's original folksy ads. Quaker tried to use Snapple to sell its blockbuster brand Gatorade. Quaker jammed monster Snapple bottles on the shelves, where they languished because customers didn't want monster bottles. Snapple distributors didn't like Quaker's marketing. Customers didn't buy Quaker's line extensions. The brand franchise began to dribble and leak away.

The Quaker Oats marketing people did not love Snapple. They did not treasure the brand's personality. They did not drink Snapple at breakfast, lunch, dinner, anytime, all the time. Quaker's marketing people looked down on the Snapple brand. Quaker big-companied, bureaucratized, and battered the Snapple brand.

Quaker sold the brand, at a big loss, to another entrepreneurial bunch of marketers, not too unlike the original founders. The new people repolished the Snapple silver. They resurrected Snapple's brand personality. They brought back the Snapple Lady. They introduced weird new flavors. They drink Snapple morning, noon, and night. Yup, the brand is back.

Quaker Oats should have known better than to dump the Snapple Lady. The Snapple Lady was part of the brand. Quaker could have gone to school on the Hamm's Beer/ Heublein fiasco. Hamm's Beer was a great midwestern brand. Their advertising featured a dancing bear. The Hamm's bear also became part of the Hamm's Beer brand. Heublein bought Hamm's Beer, hated the advertising, considered the bear to be insufferably corny, and immediately dropped the bear from all advertising. Consumers revolted. Some consumers thought that Heublein had literally changed the beer's formula. Heublein killed the brand and sold it back to its original owners at a huge loss. Not loving a brand is usually hurtful to a brand. Hating a brand is a death sentence. Heublein hated Hamm's.

Loving your brand is not a guarantee of personal success. But not loving your brand is a guarantee of lackluster performance, if not outright, dismal failure.

X

Early to Bed,
Early to Rise,
Sell Hard, and Dollarize

B en Franklin almost had it right (his famous success in business counsel was "Early to bed, early to rise, work hard, and advertise"). Although old Ben didn't exhort early Americans to dollarize, he did all right: He got his picture on the $100 bill.

Dollarization is the mathematical calculation of the dollars-and-cents value of a product. "Value" is a number (as defined in *Webster's*). Value is not a string of superlatives, such as "most reliable," "longest lasting," "leak-free." Value is only correctly expressed as a number. Therefore, buzzword expressions such as "value selling," "value proposition," and "value chain" are worthless without dollarization. Dollarization puts the buzz into the buzzwords.

The marketing superstar starts with dollarization. (See the Appendix for a step-by-step methodology and application examples.) The superstar dollarizes to help with the following:

- Determining go/no go on new products.
- Market segmentation.
- Product positioning.
- Setting pricing (to value).
- Developing product claims in advertising.
- Enabling salespeople to overcome the price objection.
- Allowing customers to understand their payback and return-on-investment in the product.

After the marketing superstar dollarizes the product, he or she starts selling, and selling hard. Superstars sell inside, persuading colleagues to sell. They sell to customers. They sell to distributors and channels. They sell influencers. They sell via advertising, direct mail, packaging, public relations, low-altitude blimps, sandwich boards, and luggage tags. They sell politely, persistently, legally, honestly, consistently, creatively, and relentlessly.

Marketing superstars sell all day, because they are early to rise. They have stamina and energy because they are early to bed.

Marketing superstars work to get those Ben Franklins *ka-chinging* into the cash register.

• XI •

Always
Price to Value

Customers don't buy products; they buy the benefits they get from the products. Customers don't wake up in the morning and say, "I've got $10,000. Let's buy some bearings or drills or gaskets or glue or water pumps!" Rather, the customer has a problem (a.k.a. a need) and wants to solve the problem. The customer may need to get new consumers into her dress shop, so she invests not in a newspaper ad, but rather in the newspaper circulation that reaches and attracts her potential consumers. The customer may need holes, so he buys a drill. The customer needs 1,000 holes an hour. The price the customer is willing to pay for a 1,000-hole-an-hour drill is based on the value of getting 1,000 holes, or the cost consequence of not getting the holes. Determining the value of 1,000 holes to the customer is where the super marketer starts. To determine a potential starting price, you must dollarize the value of 1,000 holes. If each hole is worth 10¢, then the buyer will be willing to pay up to $100.

Price your products or services according to the value the customer receives from the product. Do not price your product based on its production cost plus a markup. Do not price your product solely according to supply and demand. (Even the most basic commodities can be differentiated and priced to value. And gouging customers who need plywood during a hurricane may produce short-term profits but will long be remembered by the customer base.) Do not automatically price your product to mirror competitive pricing. Do not price your product below cost.

Pricing to value is a marketing strategy. This strategy is grounded in understanding the customer. Pricing to a target gross margin is a manufacturing cost-recovery strategy and has nothing to do with the customer or the marketplace. Invariably, target gross margin pricing, which is by far the most common approach, misprices the product, often forfeiting significant profit. Manufacturing-driven companies often automatically pass any improvements in cost on to the customer via lower price. There are times when competition makes this practice necessary. But it should never be automatic. In pricing to value, manufacturing costs are irrelevant. It doesn't matter if you make the product at zero cost. You price to value. If your price to value is lower than the cost of manufacturing, drop the product from your line. If it is a new product and cost exceeds value, don't launch. Kill the product.

Pricing to value requires good customer knowledge, dollarization skills, and courage. Most marketers are afraid to price the product to its real value. They're afraid the price is too high. They don't know how to defend the price with the sales force (too many of whom prefer to sell on low price), or with the trade (which does not know how to sell value). The marketing superstar does not fear the price. The marketing superstar constantly educates the sales force, the channels, and the marketplace to the real value of the product.

When customers understand the dollarized value, price is just a detail.

• XII •

The Folly
of Price Cutting

*P*rice cuts do not stimulate derived demand (see Chapter
XV). Price cuts are followed by competitors. Price cuts
start price wars. Wars wound and kill. Price wars wound or
kill all combatants.

Cutting price instantly cuts profit, because costs stay the
same. (Some price cutters argue that the increased volume
will reduce some costs. Increased volume from a price cut
only happens when your product is priced above its real or
perceived value and customers respond accordingly. A perma-
nent price cut below marketplace pricing does not increase
profitable volume.)

A McKinsey study shows that, on average, a 1 percent cut
in price reduces operating profits by 8 percent, assuming no

increase in unit volume. This means that if your price is $1.00, and the sales force wants to cut the price to 99¢ ("it's just a penny!"), the impact will be a sharp reduction in profit. A similar study of more than 500 companies across a mix of industries shows similar impact: The following chart illustrates the relative impact of a 1 percent improvement in fixed cost, unit volume, variable cost, and price. *Improving price yields the greatest impact on operating income.*

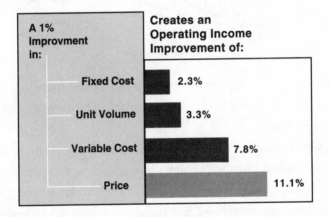

This next chart shows the increase in unit volume needed to break even (on contribution dollars) after a price cut. The various curves represent different levels of Gross Margin percentage. (Gross margin is selling price minus cost of production.)

For example, if a seller whose original price generates a contribution level of 25 percent agrees to cut his price by 15

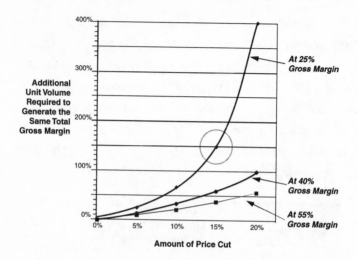

percent, he would have to sell 150 percent more units to generate the same total contribution dollars as he earned before the price cut.

Good competitors don't compete on price. They compete on product quality, product innovation, service differentiation, advertising creativity, salesmanship, technical service, store location, merchandising skill, and employee attitudes. Good competitors strive to provide value and believe in pricing to value. Good competitors sell products that vary in value and price, but they do not senselessly cut price.

Price cutting is price-a-cide.

A
Price-to-Value
Parable

*T*his story may be apocryphal, but it is valuable none-
theless.

Pablo Picasso, the painter, was dining at a fancy restaurant
in New York City. A fan, feeling prominent enough socially to
introduce herself to Mr. Picasso, did precisely that. Standing
by Picasso's table, the socialite gushed how thrilled she was to
meet the great artist; how she loved his work; and blah-blah-
blah. Encouraged by Mr. Picasso's polite acceptance, the fan
begged, "Oh, Mr. Picasso, would you draw me a sketch?"

Picasso grabbed some paper, and with pen and pencil,
promptly sketched the waiters passing parfaits.

As the woman reached for the sketch, Pablo Picasso said,
"Madame. That will be $10,000." Shocked, she replied, "But

that only took you five minutes." "No, Madame," replied
Señor Picasso, "it took me fifty years."

Pablo Picasso priced his product to its value, not to its
cost of manufacture. He priced his product to its investment
value, not to the sum of the cost of the paper plus the ink plus
some hourly wage rate. A painting with the brand name
"Picasso"—in signature form—is worth more than a similar-
looking painting with the name "McGillicuddy."

Determine your product's economic value to the customer and price the product to that value, not to the manufacturing cost.

Learn pricing—if not painting—from the Master.

· XIV ·

Always Sell
Consequences

*C*ustomers would rather not lose something than save
something. If offered the choice to not lose $100, or to
save $100, the customer will choose the not lose option. This
is an important marketing understanding. Always communicate the consequences to the customer of going without your
product. The fear of loss is a much stronger buying motive
than the potential to save.

For example, take the storm window manufacturer who
claims its double-paned windows "Will save you $2.00 a day
in reduced energy consumption." It is more effective, more
memorable, and more compelling to say, "You are losing $720
a year with your old single-pane windows. Try ABC Double-
panes." The gauge and controls company that says, "New

Spillex Controller prevents overfilling, saving you hundreds of dollars in cleanup costs," would generate more inquiries and more sales using, "Overfilling spills your dollar bills on the ground. New Spillex Controller stops your loss."

Every benefit for every product can be dollarized. Every benefit for every product can be expressed in the dollars and cents it delivers to the customer. Every benefit can be calculated to show the economic value to the customer. The benefit can be presented as a saving for the customer, or as the cost of going without the solution.

It is always more effective to influence the customer by showing the cost of going without, along with any other consequences of not buying your product. Few customers knowingly ignore consequences and then deliberately buy an alternative product just for a lower price.

The super marketer dollarizes the product benefits and then shows the customer what it is costing him per year, per week, per hour to go without the product.

Fewer than 5 percent of all marketers ground their product claims on benefits to the customer. Fewer than 1 percent of all marketers dollarize the value of their product and sell with numbers. Only the super marketer dollarizes and sells on the consequences of not buying.

Customers don't want to lose. Do customers a favor: Warn them what they will lose if they don't buy your product. When they buy, everybody wins!

• XV •

Derived Demand
Is Not
Direct Demand

*D*emand is a measure of how much of your product your customers want. (Supply is a measure of the availability of the product to satisfy market demand.) Direct demand is driven by end customers who consume the product and do not use it for any type of resale. The family that buys cornflakes and eats cornflakes is part of the direct demand served by cereal companies. Derived demand is the purchase need of customers who use the product as a component, or as part of the manufacturing of a product for resale. For example, the lawn mower manufacturer who buys wheels and motors and handlebars (to build lawn mowers) represents derived demand to wheel makers.

Understanding the difference between direct demand and

derived demand is critical. Companies selling into direct demand markets can influence that demand with advertising, promotions, coupons, price-offs. Direct demand is typical for a consumer products company. The direct demand consumer decides for herself whether she needs or wants to buy food, beverages, clothes, appliances, or vacation trips. The direct demand marketer's success potential is based on the number of consumers. (This is why consumer products marketing is driven totally by demographics.)

The marketer selling into derived demand markets cannot influence demand. The lawn mower wheel maker cannot make more consumers buy lawn mowers. The lawn mower wheel maker depends on the lawn mower manufacturer for demand. If the lawn mower manufacturer isn't selling any lawn mowers, the lawn mower wheel maker is sucking swamp water.

When a derived demand marketer cuts price, customer demand is unaffected. If the lawn mower manufacturer is not selling lawn mowers, the manufacturer is not going to buy wheels no matter what the price. When derived demand marketers cut price, they cut revenues and profits.

Too many companies do not understand their demand dynamics. If they did, they would not cut prices in the face of softening demand or a slowdown. Cutting prices is almost always a bad move in a slow market. When a direct demand marketer cuts price to gain business, the cuts are copied by competitors. When one airline cuts its fares from one city to another, the price cut is immediately matched by the competing airlines. When one of six gas stations on the street cuts its price, the other five stations cut their prices. This is good for consumers but dramatically hurts company profits and does not change market shares.

Marketing superstars understand demand dynamics. Unlike weak players, marketing superstars do not react to softening demand with price cuts. They are not the first in their industry to cut prices (although they do lead with price increases). Superstars plan and execute to increase market share by outselling and outpromoting, not by underpricing their competitors.

Fifteen Super Marketer
Must-Knows

1. The single most important ingredient for a successful business is having a customer. A customer is
   more important than the business idea, the technology, financing, management, or anything else.
   Marketing superstars get and keep customers.

2. Customers (people) buy to feel good, or to solve
   a problem. Customers value the solution to a
   problem in two ways: as the avoidance of loss, or
   as the potential for gain. The loss avoided, or the
   gain, can always be expressed as a dollar value. So
   make people feel good, and give them a real and
   perceived dollarized value greater than your
   price, and you will sell all you make.

3. People don't buy products. They buy what they get from the product. People don't buy saws, they buy cuts. People don't buy chlorine, they buy clean pools. Sell the dollarized value of the accurate cut and the clean pool.

4. It is marketing's responsibility to dollarize the value of every product benefit and every product point of difference.

5. Markets (customers) are *who* buy. Products are *what* they buy. Applications (product benefits and uses) are *why* they buy. Consequently, every marketing strategy and program must encompass all three who, what, and why elements.

6. A good way to organize and segment customers for marketing direction is to group them as "aware users," "aware non-users," and "unaware." A good use of time is to ask the aware users why they bought, and to ask aware non-users why they did not. Then wrap the answers into strategies to keep the aware users, to switch the aware non-users, and to attract and get the unawares.

7. Product quality is a marketing responsibility.

8. Direction to research and development is a marketing responsibility.

9. Sales is a marketing responsibility. Marketing's job is to show the salespeople where to walk and

to arm them to sell. Sales management's job is to be sure the salespeople walk. Hire salespeople who run.

10. You can immeasurably increase revenues if you train your sales force how to pre-plan a sales call; how to ask questions, including asking for the order; and how to listen to the customer's answer after each question is asked.

11. Salespeople will greatly increase their sales if they do two things: (a) always show the customer the dollarized value of the product's benefits over the entire life use of the product; and (b) on every sales call, ask for the order, or for a commitment to an action that leads directly to an order.

12. The three most important words in marketing strategy are execution, execution, and execution. If a marketing idea is important, then every single detail in the execution of that idea is important.

13. Brand names are intellectual assets, often more valuable than tangible assets. The Coke brand, for example, is worth more than all of the Coca-Cola Company's physical plant and equipment assets. Treat great brand names like great paintings; great brands are priceless.

14. Every product is branded. The brand name might be A280-16-2PD, a lousy brand name, but a name

nevertheless. Always use good, customer-tested, on-strategy brand names.

15. Technology does not sell; marketing sells. The equation for success for technology-based new products is 2 percent technology and 98 percent marketing. Don't depend on fantastic new technology to sell itself. Nothing sells itself.

· XVII ·
Some Rules for Choosing a Brand Name

*B*usiness-to-business marketers, start-up companies, and even technology-based companies are realizing more and more what consumer packaged goods companies have known since 1900: Brand names are important; so important they are often a company's most valuable intellectual asset. However, many companies do not have the resident brand name development expertise required to do a good job on this important strategic issue. All too often, companies name their products based on internal schemes (such as numbering systems) or on acronyms that shorthand some company jargon. Here are a few guidelines to use when conceptualizing and naming new products and services.

1. Ultimately every product gets a name—it might be a number or a code, but it's a name—so why not give it a good name: a name that helps get and keep customers.

2. Do not use the product or service category as the brand name. For example, "high-resolution television" or "low-cal ice cream" are not brand names; they are product categories.

3. Don't name the product with initials, especially initials that are an abbreviation for internal jargon. Let the marketplace choose to use the initials (e.g., ESPN).

4. Whether you "like" or "dislike" the brand name is not a criterion for choosing the name. Brand naming is not a popularity contest among managers.

5. The primary criterion for a brand name is the product's positioning. Positioning is, in itself, an intellectual marketing exercise of the highest order. Many companies, including advertising agencies, do not really understand the concept of positioning. Positioning starts with an understanding of your target segment and knowing your customer's perception of competitive substitutes.

6. Consequently, when judging whether a proposed brand name is "on or off strategy," you are really

judging the name against a very carefully constructed and customer-tested positioning statement. (Examples of good positioning statements are "TV dinner," "automated teller machine," "tubeless tire.")

7. Brand names that link the product to a product category or benefits are good (e.g., Pampers, Loctite, Reflexite, Sealed Air, Timex, Bufferin).

8. Brand names consistent with key product benefits are good (e.g., Healthy Choice, Surge).

9. Names that reinforce a brand personality and tone are good (e.g., Obsession perfume).

10. Some brands with strong marketing generate customer-created nicknames that themselves become brand names (e.g., McDonald's = Mickey D's; Budweiser = Bud; United Parcel Service = UPS).

11. Sometimes a brand name that is nontraditional for a product category or industry will stand out and reduce the cost of creating awareness (e.g., Apple Computer, Ben & Jerry's Ice Cream, Snapple, Yahoo).

12. Brand names don't have to mean something (e.g., Kodak, Advil, Exxon).

13. Brand names should be memorable, pronounceable, legally available, and readable.

14. Always test a brand name for negatives. Certain words trigger unexpected customer negatives. The wrong word could trigger confusion, distaste, or anti-use sentiments. For example, a proposed brand name, "Stick-it," for a glue pencil caused some prospective customers to think of needles, stabbing, and less-than-polite street gestures. The proposed brand name "Pop Tails" for a soda-flavored alcoholic beverage confused customers. They didn't know if the product was a soda pop or a mixed cocktail. A major running shoe company introduced a sneaker aimed at women. Unfortunately the brand name, "Incubus," is also the name of an evil spirit that violates sleeping women! That brand was quickly put to sleep.

15. A good brand name will not sell a bad product. But a good product with lots of marketing support can build a so-so brand name into a franchise.

• XVIII •

Always Put the Brand Name in the Headline

*A*dvertising messages must be grounded in the benefits of the product. The subject of the ad is the hero of the ad. Always put the name of the hero in the headline, or in a prominent subhead. Always put the brand name or company name or both where your customer will see it—in the headline. Ad headlines without the brand name are like a business card that has "Me" instead of the card bearer's name. Ad headlines without the brand name are unadvertising. Ads without the brand name in the headline are a waste of money.

Advertising agencies hate this rule. This rule, they sneer, fetters creativity. The brand name may be too long, too cumbersome, too plain. Brand names too often get in the way of the clever, witty phrase. So, the advertiser leaves the brand name out of the headline. The brand name is then buried in the copy, waiting to be discovered by the customer so enthralled and compelled by that cute headline that she rushes to read the rest of the ad . . . which never happens!

Perchance, there is that one-in-a-thousand headline with no brand name that does get the customer to read or watch or listen to the whole ad or commercial. And, perchance, the customer does read the hidden brand name. If this happens, ultimate brand recall will be low to nonexistent. This is because the second and third and tenth time the customer sees the ad, the customer will remember having read the ad, will continue on, not bothering to reread, and therefore will miss the brand name. Ergo, no enduring brand recognition. Putting the brand in the headline ensures that a customer who has previously read or seen the ad will at least see the brand name again.

This brand name headline rule is crucial for billboard advertising, yet therein the rule is often violated. Driving by at fifty-five miles per hour, surrounded by road ragers, the consumer has only a glimpse to absorb, not to read, your message. No one glimpses a billboard and thinks, "What a great message. Let me pull over to the side of the highway and read this billboard." Put up your brand name or logo or both.

Alas, one can hear the plaintive wail from the uncreative advertising agency legions reminding all of the famous Apple "Automaton" commercial that appeared just once (during a

Super Bowl) and imaged the brand only at closing. But the Apple brand was in the headline, as the entire commercial was a headline. Recall all those dippy and dopey dot-com commercials in the late '90s? They all were Apple commercial wannabes. They all burned shareholders' money. Every dot-com company was trying so hard to be edgy, cool, and hip. Most of the commercials were ego trips for the agencies and the marketers. Some of the commercials were so cool they never communicated a company name. Nearly all of the commercials failed to communicate relevant product benefits or reasons to buy. What a surprise to learn all of those nincompoop marketers are out of business.

Can you imagine an emcee introducing the honored guest speaker as follows, "And join with me, ladies and gentlemen, to welcome . . . Him"? That's a headline without a brand name.

Marketing superstars turn brand names into stars. Consider, "With a name like Smuckers, it has to be good." No ducking, bobbing, or weaving with that brand name. Just a great headline and slogan.

The marketing superstar loves the brand; he is the custodian of the brand. Put the brand name in your headline. Your brand needs constant reinforcement. If you bury your brand name, you will bury your brand.

• XIX •

Never Use "We"

Never use the personal pronouns "I," "me," "we," "us," or "our" in advertising, packaging, sales literature, or anywhere else in marketing communications. "We" is about the marketer. Customers don't care about the marketer; they care only about themselves. "We" is in the first person. The only person that is first to the customer is the customer. "We" is a bad proxy for your brand name or company name. Your job is to build brand awareness, not to build "we" awareness. "We" can be any brand, any company. "We" means nothing.

Never use "we," "us," or "our" in the headline. The advertisement is not about you, it is about the benefits of your product to your customer. When an advertiser uses "we" and not the brand name, the company must assume that the customer already knows the company, or instantly recognizes the company. If the customer already knows the brand message, then why advertise at all? "Brand awareness" advertising means keeping customers aware of the brand, not of a personal pronoun.

Here are two key research findings: (1) in head-to-head comparisons, the ad featuring the brand name in the headline generates higher brand recall than the same exact ad using "we"; (2) copy written in the first person is perceived by customers as self-serving and not objective. Conversely, copy written in the third person is perceived as more objective.

Putting "we" in the headline is no different from substituting "we" for your company name on corporate signage, on stationery, or in the Yellow Pages. You wouldn't spend money and erect a huge sign in front of your building that says "Our World Headquarters." You wouldn't put "Me" on your business card and omit your name. So, don't do it in advertising or anywhere else.

· XX ·

What, Pray Tell,
Is the Difference?

"**O**ur people make the difference," pretentiously proclaims one company after another. Oh, really? And what is the difference the people make? If the "difference" is your selling point, then articulate that difference.

Pick up a handful of magazines and whip through the ads. In one ad, you will be told, "The right broker makes all the difference." Not just *the* difference; *all* the difference. Does the wrong broker not make a difference? In another ad, you will learn, "In Winemaking As In Nature, It's The Smallest Details That Make The Difference." My, my! The smallest details! Not the attention to the details, just the details themselves. (In this ad, not only do you never find out the "difference," the brand name of the product is not mentioned. That is one small detail the advertiser might reconsider adding.) In another, you will be exhorted to "Volunteer to Make a Difference!" (One infers that the exclamation point is supposed to make this claim more important.) And you will be counseled, "The right choice makes the difference," because you certainly would not want to make the wrong choice. And when it comes to choice, how about the marketer who prints, "Your car choice makes a difference," on the lid of a yogurt package! Difference is everywhere: "You can make a difference in people's lives," "feel the difference," "experience the difference," "you'll see the difference night and day," and a hundred other variations of the same theme in the slogans and ad headlines of lazy marketers.

Such marketers are too lazy to dig, and study, and think, and write and rewrite until they can crisply state whatever their product's "difference" actually is. Look around. Read the ads, listen to the slogans, look at truck side panels. Everybody is "doing the difference." Not only is this lazy marketing, it is myopic. Don't those advertisers notice that with everyone claiming "difference," they all are the same?

The super marketer knows how his or her product is different and states that difference. If the product difference is more peanuts in a candy bar, the advertising doesn't say "chew the difference" or "crunch the difference." The super marketer's ads and sales literature and packaging and selling story all say, "Chunk-a-Choc candy bar has 14% more peanuts than any other candy bar." If the product difference is a dishwasher that lasts longer than any other, the marketing superstar's ads don't say, "Our rinse cycle makes the difference." Instead, the ads claim, "Greatplate dishwasher will run for eight years, two more years than other dishwashing machines."

One can almost feel sorry for the boutique New England dairy trying so hard to be a modern old-fashioned alternative to the big milk sellers. The New England dairy has old-style returnable glass milk bottles and hip strawberry and chocolate flavors. They have old-style caps and a clean look. One mom gave the brand a shot, buying three bottles. Must have been a bad batch, summer heat, cranky cows, or something, for each bottle—white, strawberry, and chocolate—had turned, gone sour, congealed, coagulated. But how could that be? For smack on the front of the bottle the dairy boldly brags, "Taste the difference quality makes." There's no use fretting over spoiled milk. But someone should be anguishing for the money wasted on such a trite slogan. It is udder nonsense.

You must understand your product's point of difference and factually state the difference(s). Use numbers. Provide the customer with facts and data. Let the customer decide if your factual statement is a compelling and relevant difference.

If your customer knows the competitor, she will recognize your factual claim as a point of difference. If the customer does not know the competition, and your factual claim resonates, she might investigate your product first. When she does investigate your product, you can make the sale.

• XXI •

Never Use Bad Words in Advertising or Selling

*E*verybody knows the good words to use in advertising: "new," "free," "try," "you," "discover," "introducing," "now." But not everyone knows the bad words in advertising and selling, or they wouldn't use them. Ninety-nine percent of the time when these bad words are used, they are meaningless.

BADDIES	EXPLANATION
We, me, I, our, us	Customers care only about themselves, not the seller. Use the brand or company

BADDIES	**EXPLANATION**
	name instead of a personal pronoun. Write copy in third person.
Difference	See Chapter XX.
Solutions	What else are you selling if it is not a solution to a problem? State your solution. For example, if your product solves a leakage problem, say, "Dripstop eliminates leaks." The customer will decide if it is right for him.
Quality	Every product has quality, from poor to great. Quality is defined only by the customer, not the marketer.
It	"It" means nothing. "Coke is it." Coke is what? Coke is delicious? Coke is Pepsi? Coke is not Pepsi? Tell the customer what "it" is. (Coca-Cola can, because of enormous brand awareness, get away with such

BADDIES	EXPLANATION
	an empty and vague slogan, but no other company can.) To wit, what does this headline from a prominent HMO mean: "We take *it* personally."
Technology	Everything sold depends on some kind of technology. There is no "high tech." There is old tech and new tech. Making cymbals uses 300-year-old technology. Making wine combines 1,000-year-old technology with modern invention. Customers don't buy technology. They buy what they get from the technology. No one cares how a fax machine works. No one cares how a cell phone works. But people buy millions of both.
Lifetime	As in "lifetime guarantee." Lifetime of a moth, or Methuselah, or the selling company? Take your pick.

BADDIES	EXPLANATION
Source	As in "we are the source" or "come to the source." Source of what? State the source if you think that will positively influence the customer.
Superlative adjectives (e.g., most, best, superior, optimize, minimize, fastest, lightest)	See Chapter XXII.

One company took a deep breath, ordered a drumroll, and attempted to say nothing in a fancy corporate-speak way. The company succeeded. Their headline takes the reader's breath away: "Our superior technology + Our outstanding quality = Solutions that make a difference." Huh?

· XXII ·

Advertise and Sell with Numbers, Not Adjectives

R ead any company's brochures, literature, and advertising. Review sales presentations. You will find endless product claims all saying how great the product is. Products are glowingly advertised as lighter, faster, warmer, cleaner, better. Products maximize, minimize, optimize. Products are superior, most reliable, longest lasting, most durable. Products will save money, save energy, save time, reduce scrap.

But what does the customer know after reading that a product "cleans in less time than other detergents," or "frees up more time in the workday," or "speeds up assembly time"? What do "less," "more," and "speeds up" mean? How much "less"; how much "more"? Is "less" five or fifty? After reading adjective-based product claims, the customer knows nothing!

Instead of empty adjectives to sell your product, use numbers. Use facts and data. Let the facts speak for themselves. The customer will understand.

For example, it is common to see or hear or read an advertisement that claims, "Based on recent head-to-head comparisons, ABC brand outperformed all other leading brands." "Outperformed" does not inform the customer. It is better to claim, "ABC brand did not fail after 1,000 hours in a 500° test oven. All other brands failed in less than 700 hours." Instead of claiming "Brand X is most reliable," say, "After 1,000,000 starts and stops, Brand X stays maintenance-free."

The customer is bored to death with self-serving superlative product adjectives. The customer is inured to the superlatives and ignores them. The customer has heard every claim in every way. Facts are different. Customers like different. Customers like facts, because they like to decide for themselves. Facts sell.

Imagine this exchange between a National Football League coach and a sports agent trying to sell a client, a prospective player, to the coach:

> **Agent:** "Coach. You've got to sign this kid. He's fast."
> **Coach:** "How fast?"
> **Agent:** "Really fast! And he's big and strong!"
> **Coach:** "How big?"
> **Agent:** "Really, really big!"

After this exchange the coach knows nothing! The good agent, the good advertiser, the rainmaker, the marketing superstar would say: "Coach. You've got to sign this kid. He runs the 40-yard dash in 4.4 seconds. He's 6'4", 250 pounds, and can bench-press 500 pounds. Can we set up a time for you to give him a trial?"

Don't advertise and sell using *Roget's Thesaurus*. Use numbers, not narrative. Use facts, not fantasy. Don't sermonize; advertise.

• XXIII •

Don't Put Your Phone Numbers on Your Trucks

*O*ne of the most common marketing mistakes is putting telephone numbers, and not town names, on delivery trucks and vehicles. This is a waste of money. People can't and don't write down numbers. Area codes are always changing, necessitating either costly repainting or driving with an obsolete number. The only time people write down a company's number is when the truck driver has forced them off the road or spun a stone into their windshield. Often marketers exacerbate the mistake by painting the ten-digit phone number in a dominant size, trying to do the wrong thing right.

It is more effective to feature your company name, your town and state, and a good advertising line.

There are some exceptions to this rule. If your vehicles

provide a daily or consistent consumer service, and that service is provided locally, such as a taxi service, it is okay to display a seven-digit (not ten-digit) number. It would be best if the number were easy to remember, such as 777-7777.

Another exception is if your number, when expressed in letters, is a memorable word or phrase. This is far less often the case than most marketers think. If the spelled-out number is your company name, and you run the digits beneath the name, you reinforce brand awareness, though minimally. If your company sells electronic bug zappers, 1-800-ZAP-BUGS (with the 1-800-927-2847 run beneath) is good. Other good examples are 1-800-Loctite (the brand name) and 1-800-Sandvik (the company name). The number 1-800-GoFedEx is not as good, but it is acceptable (the "Go" is forced). These examples work because the company's phone number, in effect, either is a proxy for the brand name or acts as an ad headline.

Your truck is not a phone book. Your truck is a moving message board. Your company name, your business, and your town are the messages that matter.

Keep on truckin'!

Don't Hit Into
a Triple Bad Play

A Case History

An observant fellow casually waits at a red traffic light. Through the intersection, the first truck flashes past. The fellow reads the company slogan, "Make the precision difference" but cannot catch the whizzing ten-digit telephone number. "Darn," murmurs the fellow to himself. "I so wanted to make the precision difference." A second truck passes, and the light turns green.

The fellow follows the second truck. The rear panel of the truck is a type of billboard. It is a billboard because it displays an advertising slogan. The target audience must be that infinitely small number of random drivers (and, it must be assumed, other front-seat passengers) unluckily trapped just behind the truck. After all, no other drivers can see the slogan, let alone read it. The company that owns the truck (and the company is a huge, multinational, top-notch consumer package goods marketing company) now has the hapless driver/consumer locked behind in a "read our ad" position. The ad slogan is printed in small, hard-to-read letters. (The company must believe in discreet, not too pushy communication.) Or perhaps that's why the truck driver drives slowly . . . so the car driver can get close and read and absorb and get sold by the compelling ad copy.

The hard-to-read advertising slogan, bouncing, moving, smeared with road dirt, says "We All Make a Difference."

Luckily for the advertiser—the owner or leaseholder of the truck—the unlucky following driver/consumer has twenty slow miles of "no passing" zones to read, interpret, contemplate, and grasp the advertising message. Luckily for the truck advertiser that the unlucky following driver/consumer is an observant fellow and tries a thousand times harder than anyone else on the planet to understand the message.

The advertising slogan commits a "triple bad."

1. "We." Who is "we"? Any company in the world could be the advertiser. No brand name included. No brand recognition. No brand recall. No nothing.

2. "We all." Is "we all" used instead of "some of us"? Or is the unknown company (the "we") welcoming the rest of us ("we all") open-armed into their contribution (the "difference") to humankind?

3. "Make a difference." And what—oh Lord, give us strength—difference do "we all make"? And what does it have to do with the company's product?

This advertiser, using the rear panels of lots of trucks as billboards, spent money directing the copywriter, writing the copy, approving the copy, painting the trucks . . . and every single cent was sewered.

Luckily for the advertiser, this one-in-a-million behind-the-truck driver/consumer was intrigued by the "We All Make a Difference" ad slogan and was determined to pass the truck, read a side panel, and find out the name of this difference maker.

Unluckily for the advertiser—drats! shucks! oops!—the truck abruptly turned off the road and disappeared!

Twenty slow miles of billboard advertising all for naught. Tsk! Tsk!

Three wrongs. Three outs. Game over.

• XXV •

Marketing Superstar Instant Challenge #1

Your product is an obscure, unknown dessert wine with the difficult to pronounce name Muscat de Frontignan. The dessert wine category is not popular. One of Muscat de Frontignan's points of difference is that it is the only 100 percent varietal dessert wine on the market. The wine is made exclusively with the Muscat de Frontignan grape varietal. Consequently, the wine has a pleasant, clean taste, unlike the cloying sweetness of better-known dessert wines. It also has a higher price than other dessert wines. This presents another challenge: The wine-buying segment of the population comfortable with paying higher prices for better-quality wines is composed primarily of table wine buyers, not dessert wine buyers. However, this customer is constantly on the prowl to "discover" new wines, is impressed with boutique wineries and their supposed scarcity of product, and is willing to experiment.

You convinced a chain of eight exclusive wine shops, each shop located in a tony, upscale town, to test your wine. The chain agreed to put two cases of wine (twenty-four bottles) in one store. You just received a call from the buyer who said that unless your wines start to sell, they would be returned and not carried in the other shops. It is Wednesday, and the wine buyer's deadline to see sales movement is this upcoming weekend.

Because your wine appears to be a dog with little sales revenue, your entire budget for in-store promotion is $10.

What should you do? Think about it for a few minutes. The marketing superstar's *ka-ching, ka-ching* idea is on page 147.

· XXVI ·

Don't Send
a Ransom Note

C ollect a sample of every printed communication you now send to or show customers. Get a sample of everything now in use regardless of when it was originally designed or printed. Get samples of current advertising, sales literature, billboards, product packaging, company newsletters, logos, stationery, signage, brochures, web site, Yellow Pages ads, truck or vehicle decoration, uniforms, parking passes, visitor badges, annual reports, trade show booth panels . . . everything the customer might see.

Paste each sample or photo or rendition in tight adjacency to one another on large poster boards. What does that composite visual look like? Are the colors, illustrations, images, typefaces, layouts, messages, copy style, and logos consistent and harmonious, presenting a unified look? Or does your poster board look like an amateur's ransom note: an understandable message, but one communicated in a hodgepodge of letters and graphics?

Your poster board is how your customer sees your company and your products. Each visual should reinforce the other. You must have a consistent look, a consistent trade dress. Your job is to train your customer to instantly recognize your company. You do this not by confusing the customer, but by providing a familiar, memorable look.

Your message competes with every other communication that bombards your customer daily. Don't add to the bombardment by sending multiple looks. Instead of sending two or three or ten different images to the customer, send ten of the same images. United Parcel Service (UPS) is a master at presenting one image. Their brown trucks and brown uniforms and brown planes are ubiquitous and instantly recognizable, strengthening and reinforcing brand awareness.

Consistency of look does not mean you can't change. You can change. You probably should change. But once you change your trade dress, change everything to match.

The Betty Crocker cake mix label and Aunt Jemima maple syrup label have changed through decades but have not confused the consumer. Black Velvet Canadian Whisky has been using different Black Velvet models in advertising and in-store promotion for thirty years. But the Black Velvet "look" stays the same, continuously building brand awareness, brand recognition, and brand recall.

Sending a ransom note will get your company's growth rate arrested.

• XXVII •

Be Your Own Customer

*T*here is no better way to follow the cliché "Stay close to your customer," than to be your customer. Experience doing business with your company as much as possible, the same way your customer does. Read your company's product advertising and sales literature. Have a non-knowledgeable friend read the advertising. Is it clear, straightforward, devoid of technical jargon, devoid of industry lingo? If you are not familiar with the assembly instructions that accompany your product, give them a try. If you are familiar with the assembly, ask a non-technical person to do the assembly.

Call your 800 number. Call with a tricky question, one you discovered reading customer complaint letters or reading quality surveys. How long does it take to get connected to a person? What do you think of the tunes played while you wait? Does the person you're connected to have the authority to solve your problem? If you get the problem solved, or if you don't, call back and do it all over again. See if there is a difference in outcome from the two calls. (Make three or four calls if you really care.)

Fill out your advertising inquiry cards and monitor the response. Fill out a business reply card and monitor the response. Fill out one of your post-purchase customer survey forms. Put a note on the bottom of the form saying, "To anyone reading this form: You, or the charity of your choice, will get $25.00 if you call me. My number is . . ."

Read any and all customer complaints. Read old ones. Call the customers. Try to read and remember the phone numbers on your trucks while they are moving and you are moving. Speed past your billboard and then ask a passenger to quote the billboard message.

Visit the stores or dealerships or outlets that sell your products. Check the pricing, display, and literature of your product. Ask the clerks some questions. Buy the product, finance the product, fill out rebate coupons and warranty cards, experience the service, return the product . . . just like your customer. Time everything. Talk to everybody. Take notes.

The objective, open-minded, keenly aware, dispassionate, ego-controlled super marketer will always find ways to make it easier and better for your customer to buy, and to continue to buy.

It is not easy to be your own customer, especially when the sales cycle is long, when the purchase involves a lot of money, or when the product or service experience is complex. Yet when it is hard to be a customer is exactly when you must be. How can you fix or improve the customer experience, get an edge on competitors, and innovate if you don't know what the customer knows? The airline executive who gets VIP service from start to finish; who never gets bumped, never trapped in a middle seat between two weight lifters; or who, as is too often the case, whistles up a private jet is not going to be in touch with what bothers the customer. The auto manufacturer executive who drives a new and different car model every day, always shined, fully gassed, who never visits a dealership to endure the hassle of price, options, colors, service, and delivery date cannot relate to the people who pay his paycheck. Do you think your doctor waits an hour in a patient waiting room when he sees his doctor? If he did wait an hour, maybe you wouldn't be kept waiting in his waiting room. (Isn't the concept of a "waiting room" obnoxious? No one should wait if they have a prescheduled appointment.)

When you are your own customer, and you are happy and pleased, your business will do well. And vice versa.

• XXVIII •

Banish
All Buying Barriers

*D*o not make it harder than it already is for your customers to do business with you. Remove all barriers
to buy, big and little. Eliminate any policy that makes things
convenient for the seller but can be a hassle for the customer.

Don't be like the dry cleaning establishment in New
Hampshire that exhibits an eyeful of signs all scolding the customer not to do this or do that. The dry cleaner warns customers that clothes left longer than sixty days will be
discarded. The dry cleaner has a sign: "We are not responsible
for zippers, cuffs, buttons, elastic, shoulder pads, beads." The
same joint has signage screaming, "We don't take credit cards"
and "We don't take personal checks." Consider the customer,
running an errand to pick up $224 worth of dry cleaning,

sent away because she did not have enough cash. After getting enough cash, she returned and gave the dry cleaning person three $100 bills, only to be challenged, "Don't you have anything smaller?" Astonished, the customer replied, "You don't take credit cards. You don't take checks. And now you don't take cash! How can I do business with you?" The dry cleaning person just shook her head at the stupidity of the annoying customer.

Review all your policies. Are any of them an obstacle to buying? A major gear manufacturer, and an excellent company, discovered they were using a forty-year-old credit check system for all new customers. The credit checking system took three to four days to okay a customer, thereby making fast purchases impossible. The issue was made manifest when a significant potential order was delayed while the gear company checked the credit of one of the five largest automakers. Maybe the automaker is a slow payer, but its credit is good! The old, slow credit checking policy was driving good creditworthy customers elsewhere.

A luxury car dealership picked up its customers' cars for service . . . but only during the car's first 36,000 miles. When the car had 36,000 miles, the dealership stopped picking up its customers' cars, inconveniencing the customers. That policy was silly. At 36,000 miles the customer is chronologically closer to buying a new car. That is precisely the time when the dealership should be showering rose petals on its customers, not shunning them. Don't make customers unhappy just before they intend to buy.

The Visa credit card organization features stores and resorts and restaurants and other places of business in its commercials and advertising. The businesses featured in the commercials brag that they accept Visa but do not accept the American Express charge card. Not accepting the American Express reduces, by one, the ways a customer can buy. If the customer faces a barrier to buy, she may go elsewhere. The argument that businesses make for not taking the card is that American Express card charges 1 or 2 percent more than other credit cards (on purchases customers make). The net difference between the cards is, say, 1 or 2 percent. One percent on a five-day, $600-per-day visit to a resort in Bermuda (one of those featured in the ads) is 1 percent of $3,000, or $30! Why would any resort that invests tons of money on advertising, glossy literature, travel agent commissions, reservation services, and employee training risk blowing a $3,000 customer visit to save $30! The ironic reality is that the resort never saves $30 on the American Express customer who goes elsewhere; it loses $3,000.

Not accepting the American Express card is dumb. Bragging about it is even dumber.

Don't be dumb. Let people buy. Be like the wonderful

folks in the Caribbean, at resorts that do take credit cards, checks, cash, conch shells. When asked for anything, the typical Caribbean answer is always, "No problem, mon."

And always have enough change in the cash register. Don't put the burden on the customer as a convenience to the merchant. Don't post little signs saying "We need ones," "We need change," "No bills over $20 accepted," "Please pay as close to purchase amount as possible." Customers don't like such signs.

Having cash in the cash register is one little way to get more cash into that register.

• XXIX •

Always Thank Your Customers

Your customers are very smart; after all, they decided to do business with you. Thank the customer. Thank the customer with sincerity. Praise the customer. Congratulate the customer. But do so sincerely. If you aren't sincere, the customer will sense cynicism, not sincerity.

There are oodles of ways to say thank you. Every product package the customer sees should say, "The employees of XYZ Corp. thank you for your business." Salespeople should send customers handwritten thank-you notes. The carpet merchant should call each customer to inquire about the carpet installation and to thank the customer. Accounts receivable managers should send a thank-you note when the tardy customer finally pays an old bill. Quality assurance people should personally respond to every complaint (and not with a trite form letter) and thank the customer for taking the time to alert the company to a problem. If it is considered a serious problem, the president, or another acceptably high ranking executive, must call the customer.

Please, no self-serving thank-yous, such as the billboards and full-page ads that proclaim, "Thank you for letting *us* celebrate our 30th year in business!" These ersatz "thank-yous" are about the advertiser, not the customer. Sometimes the self-congratulations posing as a thank-you, are nakedly self-serving. The following advertisement is a testament.

Headline: "Thanks for helping us save minds, save lives."

Visual: Alphabetical list of sponsors.

Subhead: "and by thanking you all on one page, save trees."

Copyline: "The Ad Council would like to publicly thank our sponsors who have enabled our public service campaigns to have a positive effect on the lives of millions of Americans."

This immodest ad is a boast, not a thank-you.

Imagine the same ad with the simple headline "Thank you, Ad Council sponsors, for saving minds and lives."

Give credit. Don't take credit.

The crime is that this advertiser does superlative first-class work, and its sponsors are first-class organizations. It does good work for others, but not for itself. Marketing superstars keep a grip on their egos. Some ego Super Glue is needed here.

Write a thank-you when you don't get the business. Customers will appreciate your goodwill. They will remember you the next time they are ready to buy. Your thank-you might lead to another thank-you.

Sincere thank-yous never hurt. They cost nada. Say "thank you" over and over and over.

· XXX ·

A Fast Fifteen

*H*ere are fifteen rules to remember.

1. Teaser ads are worthless. A teaser is an ad, usually one of a series, that alludes to a forthcoming product. The teaser ad does not tell the customer the product or the brand. No one cares about the tease. No one is breathlessly waiting for the surprise. No one anticipates the product. No one. Customers are too busy to care. Customers see through the artifice. Customers want advertisers to get to the point. Teaser ads are a complete waste of money. ("Coming soon" ads are not

teaser ads; they are announcement ads, announcing a product, movie, or event, and they are fine.)

2. Serve hot food hot, and cold food cold. That's the promise. That's the expectation.

3. Channels are not customers. Channels, such as distributors and retailers, are where customers go to buy products.

4. Know exactly how your company makes money. And know which products, no matter how old, make the money. Products that make money are products customers like and buy. Pour the coals to the products that ring the cash register.

5. There is always a cost to cost cutting. Know what the resultant cost is in your organization.

6. Put selling on a pedestal, not the sales force. Salespeople are critical. Great salespeople are invaluable. A rainmaker, a great salesperson, can go up on a pedestal temporarily. But not the sales force. The sales force doesn't call the shots. Marketing calls the shots.

7. If an ad doesn't sell, if it doesn't ultimately ring the cash register, it is a waste of money.

8. So-called image ads are a waste of money if they don't sell. Don't run image ads. Run ads that sell your product. Ads that sell create a positive image.

9. Superstars firmly believe that if the customer does not do business with the superstar, then both lose.

10. The end of an event is remembered more than the beginning. Always end your customer's experience so that the customer is oversatisfied, if not thrilled.

11. Sell the wine, not the winemaker. If the customer believes that product quality depends on the winemaker, the chef, or the Snapple Lady, and that persona goes to the vineyard in the sky, the customer may desert.

12. Make the customers invest something into the sales and purchase process. Get them to taste a sample; to try the product; to take the pen (as offered by the salesperson). Customers who invest buy sooner and more often than customers who don't.

13. Replace the old advertising maxim of having a Unique Selling Proposition (USP) with having a Dollarized Selling Proposition.

14. Be like the workers in the television bar Cheers. Customers go to Cheers because, as the theme song notes, Cheers is "where everybody knows your name." Customers prefer to do business with people who remember their names rather than with people who don't.

15. Mission statements must be expressed in picture words. Mission statements must be marketing mission statements. They must be expressed in galvanizing but commonplace words, not in corporate-speak. For example, note Winston Churchill's famous mission statement: "Bomb the bridges and be back safely by dawn." Or the personal computer company that works to "Put a computer in every classroom, in every household."

• XXXI •

Superstars
Love Recessions

The empirical evidence is undeniable: In every economic downturn, including the Great Depression of the 1930s, companies that outmarketed, outsold, and outpromoted their competitors emerged from the recession with increased market shares and better long-term profitability. Studies by the Strategic Planning Institute, the Association of Business Publishers, McGraw-Hill, Cahners, and Nielsen all show that marketing investments are more critical—in terms of gaining market share—during a downturn than they are when business is good. Conversely, a Mercer Co. study of 800 companies that simply cut costs in slowdowns found that 70 percent failed to get profitable growth for five consecutive years.

The marketing superstar attacks the marketplace in a downturn. The stars cut unnecessary costs, but carefully and intentionally allocate resources to acquire new customers. The companies with a hunker-down mentality cut marketing expenditures, reduce customer service staff, postpone new product launches, cut sales force commissions, and cut training. The superstars do the opposite.

During economic downturns marketing superstars employ seemingly counterintuitive strategies to get customers and to grow market share. Here is the growth approach:

- Hire newly available talent.
- Get rid of consistent underperformers.
- Maintain or increase employee training.
- Redeploy capable people into the field to sell.
- Cut customers' costs. Show customers how your products reduce waste, save time, improve warranties.
- Take advantage of the fact that customers have more time to see salespeople and a greater incentive to cut cost.
- Partner with customers to develop and launch products.
- Rush new products to market.
- Invest in web projects to cut administrative costs and reduce bureaucracy.
- Specifically target the customers of weaker or weakened competitors, especially those competitors that pull back and reduce their marketplace visibility.

- Have top managers make sales calls on end-use customers.

Recessions are market share growth opportunities. Play hardball. Be relentless. A lot of business is up for grabs. Grab it. The playing field is less crowded. Many of your competitors will adopt a "survival" approach. You must adopt a "thrival" attitude. Many of your competitors will leave the marketplace to you. Take it.

• XXXII •

Never Take
the Cheese Off
the Pizza

After 9/11, when so many airlines cut customer niceties to save costs, Continental Airlines, under CEO Gordon Bethune, did the opposite. Continental acted aggressively to attract customers. Other airlines did not. Many airlines did everything to keep customers from flying. Anti-marketing airlines "saved" money by closing ticket offices, cutting travel agent commissions, delaying terminal improvements, closing airport clubs (used by their most loyal customers), cutting food service, cutting customer service representatives, and eliminating magazines and peanuts and blankets and smiles. Those airline companies did not understand there is a hidden cost to cost cutting. The hidden cost is lost customers.

Continental Airlines feared losing market share. Keeping

or growing market share was more important to them than cutting some costs to save money. Continental accelerated terminal expansion, implemented convenient safety procedures, offered free in-flight movies, maintained most of its flying schedule, and generally devoted itself to serving customers. As Gordon Bethune put it, "Now is not the time to take the cheese off the pizza!" That's a lesson for all marketers. You can't change a declining market, but you can influence your market share.

Never cheapen the quality of your product to save money. You should work hard to reduce the cost of manufacture, to get more for your advertising budget, to get the sales force to make one more call a day. But do not cut quality or convenience or speed of delivery. And be wary of changing proven suppliers to get a substitute product at a lower price.

Changing suppliers simply to get a lower price is the hallmark of a weak marketing company. One need look only at the rise in U.S. automotive warranty claims and recalls, and the subsequent decline in market shares, to see the folly of "buy at the cheapest price." Many industry leaders, leaders in profitability, brand awareness, quality perception, and market share also have the highest cost of content. Toyota, Anheuser-Busch, Waterford crystal, Heinz ketchup, and the New York Yankees all have a higher cost of content than do their competitors. Higher cost of content to these winners results in higher profits.

When times are tough, don't cheapen and worsen your product. Don't cut your outreach to customers. The ice cream man doesn't cut back on driving to save gas. Instead, he plays "It's a Small World" louder. The marketing-minded manufacturer doesn't put a cap on sales force earnings. Instead, he gives the salespeople a bigger incentive to sell more. When times are tough, you outsell, outpromote, and outadvertise your competitor. You offer more, not less. And you never take the cheese off the pizza.

• XXXIII •

Beware the Constellation Theory of Marketing

Thousands of years ago, clever and observant Greek scholars, on warm Mediterranean evenings, lay on the grass and marveled at the heavens. They wondered, "What are those little lights up there?" They pondered. They rationalized. "That must be a chariot," one of them said. "That's the god Orion's belt," said another, "and there's a big dipper." All the Greeks agreed.

The little white lights were bears, scorpions, satyrs, and sirens. The explanations were brilliant, so brilliant that they endure today in astronomy and astrology.

But the explanations were wrong. That isn't Ursa Minor, it is a random appearance of stars.

Many companies develop marketing strategies the way the

Greeks conceived the constellations. They do it in the dark. They do it without data, without marketplace facts. These marketers don't visit the stars. They persuade themselves. They take a few bits of experience, of guess, of company myths, and they concoct a rationale for why the new product will sell or how creative the advertising is. They are like President Lyndon Johnson's war managers during Vietnam: full of complex explanations and positive predictions, but just wishes, and always wrong.

The constellation theory of marketing ensnares the bright and the busy. These managers are glib, smart, articulate, and superb at hunching the story. They are always in the office—at meetings, writing memos, giving presentations. They are not in the field, out in the marketplace getting facts. They write airtight programs based on stargazing. Because they are smart and hardworking, they have occasional success. Such success makes them certain their wrong constellation theories are right.

Professor John Quelch of the Harvard Business School surveyed consumer brand managers and marketing managers on their use of time. The survey showed the managers spent more time on "other" than "with customers." These marketing people spent more time talking with their advertising agencies than with their customers. Talking with ad agencies is fine, but now there are two groups of bright people filling the knowledge vacuum with fancy fantasy.

Marketing superstars approach the marketplace as did the original television police detective Sgt. Joe Friday: "Just the facts, ma'am." They have big marketplace ears. They listen to the customer. They have control over their egos. They don't kid themselves. If they are missing data, they admit it. They don't fall in love with their own ideas. They test their ideas with customers.

The marketing superstar doesn't look for answers in the skies unless he or she is selling helicopters or kites or paper airplanes.

Marketing Superstar
Instant Challenge #2

It is a rainy day in New York City. You are riding in a taxi on Lexington Avenue. Despite the rain there are lots of people using the sidewalks. You are bragging to a companion that you can instantly improve anyone's marketing, anyone's business. Your companion points to a shoe repair and shoe shine shop. Except for the owner, the store is completely empty. Your companion says, "How can anyone help that guy? No one's getting their shoes shined because it's raining."

You jump out of the cab and run into the store. You speak to the owner, and five minutes later people are walking in for a shoe shine.

What did you do?

The marketing superstar's *ka-ching, ka-ching* idea is on page 149.

· XXXV ·

Always Have a President's Pipeline

C ontinuous innovation, in every nook and cranny of the business, is essential for an enterprise to change, to adapt, and to go forward. The President's Pipeline is filled with innovative projects: new product ideas, new packages, new brand names, new ways to sell, new markets to enter. The President's Pipeline is not filled with the company president's ideas; it is filled with the ideas of the organization.

The President's Pipeline is usually in a notebook. The notebook contains all the projects; their priority; the people committed to make the ideas happen; schedules; and budgets.

It is called the President's Pipeline because great marketing companies revere innovation, and making innovation is a president's priority. The Pipeline makes innovation the organization's priority.

The president regularly reviews the Pipeline with those people who own the projects. The Pipeline is in constant growth: It never empties, and it can never be full. Good people want to own projects outlined in the President's Pipeline. They want to help the company and help their careers.

The President's Pipeline ensures that the company has three new products in the pantry, two on the stove, and one on the table. The President's Pipeline is the company's lifeline.

· XXXVI ·

Questions Lazy Marketers Can't Answer, but the Marketing Superstar Must

PART 1

*T*he marketing superstar must know the answers to certain critical questions. The answers are essential to proper market segmentation, product positioning, pricing, selling, advertising, and crafting marketing action plans. These questions are especially important for new products.

Lazy marketers don't know the answers, or they hunch the answers, or they ignore the questions. Lazy marketers are lousy marketers. Often lazy marketers don't know that they are lazy. Take this test and find out.

PRODUCT

1. Why was the product developed?
2. What is the product's raison d'être—the reason it exists?
3. What is the marketing reasoning behind the product?
4. How big is the market?
5. What are the product applications; how and where can it be used?

CUSTOMER

6. Why should the customer buy this product?
7. What unfilled need does the product now satisfy?
8. What objections will the customer have regarding this product?
9. What selling strategy should the salespeople use to overcome each objection?

PRODUCT BENEFITS

10. For every notable feature, answer the question "So what?" Why should the customer care?
11. What is the benefit(s) that the customer will get from each feature?
12. In specific quantitative terms, how will the customer's business be improved, and how will the

customer's personal well-being be improved, or
both?

COMPETITION

13. What is the customer using now?
14. Why is the customer buying that other product?
15. What is the disadvantage(s) of the customer's current product or the methodology that this new product overcomes?
16. What are the points of difference between this new product and the competitive offering?

VALUE

17. In dollars and cents, what is it costing the customer to go without this product?
18. How are the calculations figured?
19. Based on the dollarized value of this product, how will it be priced (to value), and what differential will that represent versus the competitive product?
20. What is the customer's dollarized return on investment?

TESTIMONIALS

21. Who else is successfully using the product—now or in the past? What are the details of that success?

22. What evidence is available to prove to the customer that the product claims are true?

You must know the answers to these questions. Your answers must be correct, thoughtful, based on facts, and homeworked. If you don't know the answers to these questions, go into the marketplace, ask and listen, do the nitty-gritty work, and get the answers. If you don't know the answers, your success is at risk. If you don't really care about the answers, you are a lazy marketer. Lazy marketers lose.

Don't be a lazy loser.

· XXXVII ·

Get Answers
to These Questions

PART 2

You must be able to correctly, objectively, and completely answer these questions. It does not matter how you get the answers. Someone else can do the research. But it does matter where you get the answers. You get the answers from customers and potential customers.

- Why do customers buy your product?
- Why do some potential customers choose not to buy your product?
- Why does the customer buy the competitor's product?
- What would it take for you to get all of a customer's business?

- What would it take for a competitor to get all of a customer's business?
- Who is/are your customer's best supplier(s) and why?
- Ask the customer, "If you were president of our company, what would you change and why?"

These questions are often best asked by an objective third party. They are hard for the marketer to ask. If the customer answers frankly, the answers are sometimes hard to hear. If the marketer asks, customers can be reluctant to answer completely and truthfully. Do not depend on the sales force to give you unbiased answers. The sales force is with customers every day, but salespeople tend to talk to people who buy, and to people they like. The sales force shies away from the tough non-buyer. The sales force answers are understandably tilted.

If you want to know the answers, don't run from bad news or knotty problems. Don't fight the findings. Fix things. Give the customers more of what they like and less of what they don't like.

Get the answers to these questions from the current customers at least once a year. Continually get the answers from new and potential customers.

· XXXVIII ·

Compete for Inches

*L*ike the professional golfer who has a teaching coach to take a quarter stroke off her game or the All-Pro wide receiver who stretches the football toward the goal line, the marketing superstar also competes for inches. Superstars work to build sales volume; to build profitable market share; to build profits; and to orchestrate thoughtful change to continuously improve the products and service. They do this in big and little ways, and they do it every day.

The marketplace is competitive. Customers want more for less. Nothing is static. Everything is changing. When the consumer goes into the store and picks the competitor's product over yours, that sale is lost forever. The marketing superstars fight for every sale.

Inches win horse races. Inches win marathons. Inches win market share.

There are countless ways to compete for inches:

- Make one additional sales call a week.
- Interview one more customer.
- Get the media to add a free commercial.
- Open the store earlier.
- Return every call.
- Ask for a commitment on every sales call.
- Get product placement in one more store.
- Get product placement on one more shelf.
- Send new product releases to five new magazines.
- Train one more distributor salesperson to sell for you on Tuesdays or Wednesdays or any day of the week.
- Ask somebody in your organization to tell you what they are doing, will do, or did today to get a customer.
- Don't waste time.
- Never let up.
- Start all over again every morning.

Don't let victory be an inch away.

Marketing Superstar
Instant Challenge #3

You have recently taken over the management of the Loondance Car Wash. You have a costly problem. Numerous customers, on a daily basis, are complaining about damage to their side-view mirrors, their bumpers, their antennas. The customers claim the damage happened when their car was in the car wash tunnel. This bothers you because you want happy customers, not unhappy customers. You are perplexed. Your people are well trained. They always push in the side-view mirrors and always alert the customers about the antennas. In addition, the entranceways to the car wash are prominently posted with several clearly painted signs warning the customer that the car wash is not responsible for damages for hanging bumpers; that certain types of cars are washed at the owner's risk; and that the car wash is not responsible for accidents to nonretractable antennas. Conversations with the prior owners and with other car wash managers were not helpful. They confirmed that constant damage claims were a fact of car wash life and should be considered a cost of doing business.

What can you do to reduce customer complaints (and, thereby, reduce customer dissatisfaction) and possibly reduce the cost of damage repairs?

The marketing superstar's *ka-ching, ka-ching* idea is on page 151.

· XL ·

Repolish
the Silver

G randma's fine old sterling silver, sitting unused in a china cabinet, darkens and blotches with time. A little polish, a little elbow grease, and the fine old silver sparkles and gleams anew. The fine old silver is just as attractive and dramatic today, after being brought out of the cabinet and back to the table, as it was on Grandma's wedding day.

Just as Grandma's repolished silver has new appeal, so, too, can old promotions, old products, and old ads. Marketers should prowl the archives and resurrect successful past promotions to see if the central idea might still be relevant. If the idea is still relevant, update the creative, rejuvenate the concept, and test the execution; if it resonates with customers, reintroduce it.

Senior, successful salespeople should remember their early days when they had few, if any, customers, little experience, and no prospects. They should remember what they did to get their success started. Did they work hard to get referrals? Did they tell every customer they met that they were in the game? Did they pre-plan every sales call and never wing it, because getting a meeting with a live customer was so rare and precious? Rainmakers remember the ways that worked in the past. They don't forget. They polish and repolish winning activities.

Sometimes companies get strategy amnesia. They forget what strategies, and what type of strategy execution, helped earn their marketplace position. These companies gradually reduce their focus on their fundamentals. They become less selective when hiring salespeople. They reduce the intensity of training. They drift from proven approaches to new product development and from proven advertising strategies. Sometimes these companies forget the importance of their old core products and get bored with them. Sometimes these companies make acquisitions so far afield from their core business that managers, successful in running what they know, become dummies running what they don't.

Marketing superstars know that old brands, old promotions, old product categories, old markets, old technologies, and old customers often mean opportunity. Old often means gold (and, of course, silver). Superstars don't care if the old idea was not their original idea. Superstars care only about building brands and building profitable sales revenue.

Just as unspoiled grandchildren, or great-grandchildren, are thrilled to receive, and then repolish, Grandma's silver, the marketing superstar is thrilled to ring that cash register with a success from the past.

Repolish the silver. *Ka-ching! Ka-ching!*

· XLI ·

First Sell Inside . . .
Always

*M*ost people, therefore most companies, do not like change. Organizations fear change and the unknown. People are uneasy with uncertainty and ambiguity. People like normalcy and predictability. This corporate and organizational mind-set is a challenge for the marketing superstar. The marketing superstar is responsible for spurring prudent change that gets the company to adapt to ever evolving markets and fickle customers.

Whereas "managers" hate ambiguity, great marketers deal with the ambiguous all the time. The marketing superstar leads the company through uncertain times and takes away corporate doubt.

The marketing superstar must convince the organization

to do something new or different, such as launching a new product. Sometimes, the marketing superstar must convince each and every part of the organization to do something that the organization may not want to do, or is not able to do, or is not ready to do. Something new to the organization, any change, means extra work for people in the organization. "New" means new tasks, requiring new approaches, new thinking, new skills. "New" means investing precious resources without certain return. "New" means risk.

Resistance to a new way is often based on valid reasoning. There are always competing points of view, legitimate and flawed. There are always hidden concerns and hidden agendas. There are always honest, risk-averse, prudent people who insist on more facts and more assurance before they will commit.

The marketing superstar treats his or her idea as a product to be sold. The customers are the people in the organization. The superstar does the homework, gets the facts, shows the economic gain represented by the idea, and shows the consequences of not going ahead. The superstar anticipates all objections to the idea and carefully plans how to neutralize the varying concerns. The superstar works one-on-one, behind the scenes, to get agreement. The superstar makes public presentations to galvanize support.

The marketing superstar does not get mad if the idea is challenged or rejected. He or she sees rejection as a request for more facts. The superstar doesn't sulk; he or she sells inside.

The marketing superstar knows there are three ultimate outcomes: (1) the company will do nothing and suffer the consequences; (2) the company will execute the initiative and will fail; or (3) the company will execute the initiative and succeed. The marketing superstar also knows that everyone will take some or all credit for success (which is fine), but no one will take responsibility for inaction or faulty execution.

To get the organization to enthusiastically adopt and execute, the marketing superstar exhibits levels of confidence that exceed levels of certainty. The marketing superstar understands the career risk associated with getting the organization to take on something new. The superstar also knows that risk is reduced with homework, fact-based thinking, creative planning, and meticulous attention to the execution of every detail. To get that cooperation, the superstar sells inside.

The marketing superstar gets cooperation and buy-in by being a "sell guy, not a tell guy."

First sell inside to get the company to sell outside.

· XLII ·

Don't Let Perfect
Be the Enemy
of Better

*I*f you have a new product ready to launch that is not yet absolutely perfect but is still better than what is on the market, introduce it. Don't postpone the launch until every little thing is fixed. Don't wait until you have the perfect product. If the new product performs a little bit better, some customers will buy that performance. Get that better new product into the marketplace fast. Beat the competition. Get an edge.

A specialty chemicals company came up with a better way to adhere ultrathin electrodes to printed circuit boards. The marketing director rushed the product to market. She knew the new product was not perfect. But the new product reduced assembly time and reduced scrap. The new product reduced the cost of producing printed circuit boards.

Two months after the product was in the market, the selling company's vice president of R&D visited the marketing director. "Catherine," the vice president stated, "I am concerned about that new PCB product. We have significant concerns about the strength of the adhesive. There are two other problems with product stability and clogging dispensers. This company has a great reputation. Why on earth did you push us to introduce a product before it was ready, before it was perfect?" The marketing director bluntly answered: "Jim, the new product doesn't have three problems. It has forty-three problems! We have to improve the packaging. The outer pack crushes in transit. Some of the directions are confusing. The rubber caps leak. The applicator clogs. The wand is clumsy to use. But the customers are buying and re-buying. We will use the sales revenue to invest in improving the product.

"And Jim," the marketing director continued, "if we had not introduced the product we wouldn't have the sales. We wouldn't have so much opportunity to improve the product. We beat the competition. The product is not perfect, but it's a winner!"

When Procter & Gamble first introduced Pampers disposable diapers as an alternative to cloth diapers, the product was not perfect. Pampers came in one size. There were no plastic tabs to secure the product. The customer needed safety pins. Pampers gradually gained market share against cloth diapers and added improvements, new features, and a variety of sizes. To enough customers, the first version of Pampers was better than diapers. Depends, for adults, is another product category made possible only by the success of Pampers.

If P&G had waited until Pampers was perfect, babies might still be wearing cloth diapers, and moms and dads would still be stabbing themselves (and their babies!) with safety pins.

Rush that better, imperfect product to market!

• XLIII •

Own a Market,
Not a Mill

*M*ills (a.k.a. factories, production plants) don't sell things; they make things. If no one sells what the mill makes, and no one buys what the mill makes, the mills stop making. A market is a customer, or any number of customers that buy or borrow or rent or lease things. Markets are the source of revenues. Mills need markets to exist.

Mills don't generate revenues; they spend money. Mills buy material, parts, labor, energy, and services. Mills are immensely important. If they don't make defect-free quality products, on time, at low costs, the owner of the mills will not stay competitive. But mills do not make money; they make things that are sold. If the products are sold at a price above cost, the company makes money.

It is the sale that makes money! Some mill managers, and some managements, mistakenly think that that mills make their company money. Mills are often critical to the ultimate making of money, but the money is only made when someone sells the product at a profit, and when the selling company collects the money.

Nike owns a market; it doesn't own any factories. Nike's products are made for Nike according to strict specifications. Nike buys its shoes from the shoe maker and resells the shoes to its markets. (Nike's shoe makers also own a market— Nike!) Dell Computer owns a market, and it sells lots of computers, but it does not make computers. Taco Bell owns a market to which it sells millions of tacos and burritos, yet Taco Bell does not make tacos.

Markets are fluid. They change in a million ways every day. Mills are hard to move. Mills can be mausoleums or monuments, as are those that line New England rivers. Mills are not fluid; they are not easily changeable. Markets want fast response. Mills move slowly.

The road to profits, to marketing success, starts with the customer, the market. The most important factor for success in business is having a customer. Markets make mills. Mills don't make markets. Mills make what markets want. When a mill makes a product without having a market, or makes what a market does not want, the results are (1) no mill revenue; (2) unsalable costly inventory; and (3) mill-a-bye-bye!

Mills and mill workers are the backbone of making things. But they do not inherently make money. If you own a mill, you should, as much as possible, treat it as a competitive outside supplier competing for your business on the basis of quality, cost, delivery, and service.

Markets—the consumers—are still buying cotton, and longtime cotton sellers are still selling cotton, but cotton mills are in mothballs.

Marketing superstars focus, focus, focus on what their markets want. If delivering what the market wants depends on a mill, make sure it's a marketing mill, not an old-fashioned manufacturing mill.

Markets, not mills, mean money in the cash register.

XLIV

Loss Leaders
Are for Losers

"Loss leaders" are products sold at a financial loss (i.e., the cost to make them exceeds the selling price) to "lead," to attract customers to the store or to the manufacturer. The hypothesis is that customers attracted by loss leaders will purchase other profitable products at the same buying moment. Actually, a loss leader is a marketing excuse masquerading as deliberate thought and strategy. Loss leader is an excuse for not being able to sell a product for a profit. Loss leader really means one or some or all of the following:

- The marketers have let the value proposition erode.
- Production costs have grown faster than price increases.
- Customers prefer an alternative product.

- The product's quality or performance is insufficient.
- The product is mispositioned.
- Sellers don't know how to dollarize the product's value.
- There has been lousy marketing: weak or nonexistent advertising, untrained salespeople, confusing brand name, bad packaging.

Selling a product at a price below the full cost of manufacturing, or below its cost of acquisition, is wrong. If the unit sale does not generate a contribution to overhead and profit, the company loses money on every sale. (Contribution is selling price minus the cost of manufacturing, or selling price minus the cost of acquisition.) The money lost on every sale is money lost forever. Contrary to business lore, the marketer cannot make up the loss with volume!

It is all right to give a product away to generate sales of another product. Such a co-promotion—for example, packaging a free paintbrush with a can of paint—is okay because the original market price of the paintbrush is not changed. After the paint can promotion, paintbrushes can be sold at the original price.

It is all right to deliberately sell a product at a loss if it is bundled with one or more products that are purchased as a unit sale. For example, the bearing manufacturer selling a set of different bearings for a transmission will include a required seal at below cost. In this case, the bearing marketer considers the cost of the seal to be a cost of the production of the bearings.

It is all right to create demand for core products by forgoing traditional margins on "host products." A host product is one that stimulates sales of profitable core products. For example, Gillette will sell razors at a close-to-cost price in order to create demand for its proprietary shaving blades. Hewlett-Packard sells its ink-jet printers at close-to-breakeven in order to create a bigger user base for its toner cartridges. These companies know what business they are in. They know they are in the blade business, not the razor business. They are in the consumable toner cartridge business, not the durable capital goods business. Consequently, zero or low returns on sales of ink-jet printers is considered a promotional expense, a marketing line item equivalent to advertising and trade shows.

These companies know what they are doing. Here is a company that didn't. The product was the beverage Finlandia. It was sold in retail stores where it was displayed in a huge pyramid fully ten feet tall. There were hundreds of bottles for sale. Bannered across the top of the display was a colorful sign: FINLANDIA FOR FREE. $8.99 WITH $9.00 REBATE COUPON!

In the state where the store was located, the marketer of the product sells to a wholesaler who sells to a retailer who sells to the consumer. Assuming the wholesaler paid the marketer $6.00 a bottle, he would add a markup and sell it to the retailer for, say, $7.80. The retailer would add a markup, say $1.19, and sell it to the consumer for $8.99. The marketer, the brand owner, would have to honor the $9.00 consumer rebate coupon. The wholesaler and the retailer would make money on every sale.

Marketers use rebates because they know only a small percentage of coupons are ever redeemed. But the redemption rate goes up as the value of the rebate goes up. Maybe 2 percent of consumers redeem a $1.00 coupon for reimbursement. But 100 percent of consumers claim the $1,000 rebate on a new automobile purchase. And large rebates are seen by customers as price cuts, not as one-time promotions. In the Finlandia case, the $9.00 rebate exceeded the retail price of the product. This meant the consumer could buy 10 bottles for $89.90 and get $90.00 back! There was no brake to limit the size of the rebate. In fact, "For Free" was an incentive to get as large a rebate as possible. And every customer who bought two or more bottles to take advantage of the rebate, claimed that rebate.

Assume the marketer's cost of making a bottle of Finlandia was $4.00. At a $6.00 selling price to the wholesaler, the marketer's contribution was $2.00 per bottle. For every rebate claimed, the marketer would lose $7.00 a bottle! This price promotion may have been a winner for the retailers, but it led to losses for the brand owner. It was a true loss leader.

There is no rationale for such a brand-debasing, money-losing, intellectually bankrupt marketing promotion.

Companies and marketing people who use loss leaders lose money. Instead of *ka-ching, ka-ching,* they hear *glub, glub.*

XLV

Marketing Superstar
Instant Challenge #4

*I*t's Friday night. You are driving home. As is the case every Friday night, you notice the flower lady's rickety roadside stand just ahead. As always, the flower lady's flowers look great. You have never stopped. You notice that, like you, few other cars stop. Suddenly the poignant voice of the late, great Phil Ochs is on the radio. Phil's song laments, "but nobody's buying flowers from the flower lady . . ." To you the song is not a coincidence. To you it is a message from the Mountain to the marketing maven. The Mountain's message is this: If you're such a hotshot marketing person, pull over and help the flower lady. You get the message. You park your car and walk to the flower lady. In addition to buying a bouquet, what's your big idea to make the bloom business boom?

The marketing superstar's *ka-ching, ka-ching* idea is on page 154.

• XLVI •

Never Run a Three-Page-Spread Ad,
or How to Burn Shareholder Money

When you read through a major newspaper or magazine and encounter a three-page advertising spread sponsored by a huge business-to-business selling corporation, the odor you smell is not fresh newsprint; it is the odor of money burning. For these advertisers are burning shareholders' money. No one reads such ads. The money invested in creating the ad and buying the media goes out in the trash . . . with the old newspaper.

There is one exception: Some customers will read three-page ads for retail establishments, in which the ad lists numerous products for sale. These ads are read primarily by women. Successful multipage ads aimed primarily at men are those that announce and list for sale vintage wine, cigars, custom-

made clothing, or auction items. These ads are actually prox-
ies for a company's catalogues.

One hilarious public burning, if you are not one of the
company's shareholders, is a four-page newspaper spread for
a consulting company. Four full-size pages! The first full page
in this ad features an extreme close up image of a deliberately
scruffy male model's face. Yuck! The only line of copy is riv-
eting: "Individually, we can achieve a lot." A meaningless,
grammatically tortured, pretentious copy line that mystifies
even the interested reader (if there were one). The second
full page of the advertisement consists of a single copy block
of nine cliché-filled sentences. Smoke pours from the page.
Flames lick at such nonsense as "method of constant dialogue
and complimentary skills interacting to create better solutions." "Solutions," one of the bad words in advertising, is
used ten times in this ad. The third full page is dominated by
an in-your-face, full-face image of a male model with half his
face scruffy, and the other half scruffier. Double yuck! The
headline tries to save Rome, "Together, the possibilities are
infinite." Get the fire extinguisher.

Full page four is all copy. Written in the first person
(another no-no!), and packed with bafflegab, the ad is now
ablaze. Wearing asbestos gloves, the reader coughs and chokes
on "results," "strategic," "integrate," "core," "technology,"
"solutions," "solutions," "solutions."

The advertiser could be arrested for attempted murder

(trying to bore the reader to death), or for starting a fire without permit or permission, or for unintentional homicide of trees.

If you run terrible ads, the newspapers and magazines and radio stations won't call you up and give you a discount because your ad stinks. Instead, they may give you some kind of readership award . . . to encourage you to keep running the ad. If your direct mail isn't effective, the post office is not going to charge you less postage. It costs as much to run good advertising as it does bad. So run only good advertising.

Clue to advertiser: When you or your agency feel compelled to run a three-page ad, it is a signal you have little to say. You have little to say, so you shout it. Rethink your creative message.

• XLVII •

Marketing Superstar Instant Challenge #5

Here is a baker's dozen of great marketing ideas. Your job is to understand why they are great. When thinking about these ideas, you should know that the first reason all of the ideas are great is because someone actually implemented them! No talk, just execution.

- Shopping carts
- American Airlines' "Frequent Flyer" awards
- Credit cards
- Baker's dozen
- Pillsbury Bake-Off®
- Infomercials
- Tupperware parties

- Microsoft's Windows® start-up screen
- De Beers's diamond distribution system
- McDonald's Golden Arch Logo
- Sears catalogue
- Vending machines
- "Don't eat meat on Friday" (an old Roman Catholic pro-hibition). Here's a hint for the last one—the original apostles were fishermen!

One more hint: *Count* the number of ideas in this list. Thirteen is a "baker's dozen."

XLVIII

Shrink to Grow

W hen business responsibilities get too big, they become unwieldy, clunky, slow, and inefficient. The twelve-person army patrol is more nimble than any army division. On a relative basis, the 300-person factory is exponentially more responsive than the 1,000-person factory. Organizations are comprised of people. People have span limits.

Shrinking sales territories spurs growth. Assume a company has set a sales growth goal of 8 percent per year. An excellent salesperson has built her territory into $2,000,000 in sales per year. For her to grow 8 percent, she must add incremental sales of $160,000. But the demands of existing customers, the smallish size of the average sale, and the length of the sales cycle all converge to make it difficult, if not impossible, for her to hit the company goal. If she does not grow her territory by 8 percent, and if her experience is mirrored by her selling colleagues, then the company will not grow 8 percent.

Shrink the territory to grow. If the salesperson's territory is reduced to $1,000,000, the 8 percent growth goal is now a much more gettable $80,000. Eight percent is 8 percent, but 8 percent on $1,000,000 is a higher probability than 8 percent on $2,000,000.

The manager who has eight people reporting to her can give twice as much attention to eight as she can to sixteen.

The ill-advised and failing acquisition that overly absorbs resources and management time will, if divested, shrink company revenues but will free assets to invest in growth opportunities. Shrink the bureaucracy. Invest the savings in growth. Shrink market segments into new niches, new spaces for your products to serve specialized customer needs. Pruning (or shrinking) rosebushes encourages future growth. Prune unprofitable customers and unprofitable products. The top line is vanity. The bottom line is sanity.

Shrink to grow can be a growth stratagem. But *you* must manage the shrinking, not your competition. Shrink to grow can shrink competitors. Don't let the competitor shrink you.

XLIX

Fill the Air
with Flailing Fists

*L*ike the savvy street fighter who throws punches from every angle hoping to land one, the marketing superstar throws appeal after appeal at the customer. The street fighter tries to overwhelm. The superstar also tries to overwhelm, to break through the protective wall of disinterest and tune-out that customers build to shield themselves from the daily commercial barrage. The boxer who falls in the twelfth round doesn't fall just because he got suddenly clobbered, but because he was pounded in rounds one through twelve. So, too, the customer who finally recognizes a product, responds to an ad, listens to a salesperson, tries a sample, or buys the product does so in response to the marketer's persistent outreach.

The marketing superstar never lets up. The superstar is

always in the game, always communicating, always selling, always contacting, always throwing leather. The marketing superstar works to build positive brand awareness, and realizing that the customer is indifferent, invests all available time, resources, creativity, and energy to reach out and persuade the customer.

Dominate the customer's consciousness and you are closer to getting and keeping the customer. Communication leads to brand recognition. Brand recognition leads to trial and usage. Usage leads to brand awareness. Brand awareness leads to a franchise. Communicate. Fill the air with flailing fists. You might hit something.

• L •

Remember Jimmy Durante

*T*he late comedian Jimmy Durante did a television bit in which he rasped, "I am surrounded by assassins." This line, or something similar, always runs through the mind of the marketing superstar. The superstar knows that competitors lurk and loom. The superstar knows that somewhere somebody is plotting to steal his customers; to make his technology obsolete; to displace his product from the shelf. The superstar knows that other companies want his market share, his store location, his brand equity. The superstar knows he is surrounded by assassins, and he works every day to prevent assassination.

Marketing superstars don't live on their laurels. They are not content. They are never completely satisfied. They stay sharp-edged. They don't take continued success for granted. They never underestimate anything or anybody. They go to bed plotting and thinking. They wake up rocking and rolling. They keep the pressure on. They are relentless.

Marketing superstars get clues from their customers and the marketplace. Customer clues keep superstars ahead of the assassins. Customers are your first line of defense against competition. Keeping customers content keeps competitors out.

Jimmy's assassins want your customers, your business. Out-work them and win.

• LI •

The First
Annual Ostrova
House Race

T his is the story of a great spontaneous marketing idea that never happened, and the lessons that were learned.

Two events were unfolding simultaneously. A company was test-marketing a new product called Ostrova. The company was trying to create a brand based primarily on an exotic look: a label featuring the prominent image of a striking, wildly bearded Russian mystery man. At the same time, a young marketing manager in the company was in the process of buying a large old house, with plans to pick up and physically move the house two miles to a new location. Moving a house is a distinctly unusual event, an endeavor unsuited for the timid. Coincidence upon coincidence, the Ostrova test market included the town in which the marketing manager's house move was to take place.

In addition to the Ostrova label on the package, the company was using billboards portraying the image of the bearded, darkly cloaked Russian mystery man as a way to attract customers. The marketing manager's idea was to wrap the entire to-be-moved house with an Ostrova billboard, complete with a large banner announcing "The First Annual Ostrova House Race." The marketing manager figured that the house move, along a major thoroughfare, would attract attention, possibly media attention, giving Ostrova invaluable publicity. To the young marketing manager the house race promotional idea was a big idea. The Ostrova brand might get television coverage, which was not part of the marketing plan, but which would jump-start brand awareness.

To the marketing manager, the "First Annual Ostrova House Race" promotion was bulletproof. The idea was unique and audacious; the move was insured; the cost was minimal; and the event would be newsworthy. To the young marketing manager, the real value of the promotion would be the fun, creativity, and excitement that would be injected into the rest of the marketing department.

Naively, as it turned out, the manager mentioned his idea over lunch in the company cafeteria. Alarmed by the conversation, a weasel in the corporate public relations department ran "upstairs" to top management to scuttle the idea. The weasel sniveled that the idea was unplanned and needed more thinking; that "first annual" couldn't be true, there wouldn't be another such event; that it wasn't a race—"a race against what?"; that it was inappropriate for the company, "not our style." And the final idea killer: The press and media might ridicule the company. Top management buckled. The weasel won. To top management it was okay for the marketing manager to take the risk of moving his house, but it was too terrifying to "race" a paper billboard up a highway. The idea killers killed. The marketing manager was told there would be no Ostrova House Race.

The day the house was moved must have been a slow news day, or maybe such a rare and unusual event was interesting. The house move, including helicopter video, made the local and regional evening television news, as well as the front page of the paper. The Ostrova mystery man never made the media. The Ostrova mystery man stayed a mystery. The Ostrova brand never generated a level of awareness to establish a franchise. Ostrova failed.

The young marketing manager learned that idea killers are clever. The killers always use arguments that seem sound, that appear to make sense. The marketing manager resolved never again to be denied by the tyranny of the timid. The marketing manager resolved that in the future, if he had an idea that would help his brand, and if the idea was within the budget, and did not break the laws of God or man, he would execute the idea.

Not doing something is easy. Executing for success is riskier. But doing nothing gets you nothing. Marketing superstars evaluate the idea, pre-test the idea, and then meticulously execute the idea. That's why superstars win . . . and weasels waffle.

• LII •

Marketing Superstar Instant Challenge #1 Answer

*T*he Muscat de Frontignan marketer used a 3 × 5 recipe card and hand-made a shelf-talker (a little sign that is attached to a store shelf). The hand-lettered shelf-talker read as follows:

Rare Muscat de Frontignan
100% Varietal
Only one bottle to a customer, please.

Within hours the store sold out. "Rare" implied "uncommon," and the wine was, therefore, a "discovery." The description "100% Varietal" meant good quality. The "one-to-a-customer" signaled scarcity, a bit of rationing. The shelf-talker's offer was the right formula to attract the "first-to-know" wine buyer. The next week Muscat de Frontignan was in all eight of the chain's stores.

LIII

Marketing Superstar
Instant Challenge #2
Answer

*T*he shoe shine store operator put up a hastily scrawled sandwich board on the sidewalk. The sign alerted customers to the consequences of going without his service. The sign's message also offered an immediate customer benefit. The sandwich board shouted:

ACID RAIN!
SAVE YOUR SHOES.
GET A SHINE.

· · ·

Ask about the Rainy Day Special

The "Rainy Day Special" was a rain check (naturally) offering a "Sunshine Shine" for $1.00 to each customer who got the rainy day shine. The promotion rang the cash register. Even more important, the shop owner gained numerous new customers.

LIV

Marketing Superstar
Instant Challenge #3
Answer

The Loondance Car Wash manager removed all the warning signs. He removed car wash signs disclaiming responsibility for this and that. He took out all negative words. The words "can't," "don't," "won't," "not," and "no" were gone. If an instructional sign was needed, its tone was changed from negative to positive. For example, "Don't stop here" was changed to "Please keep moving."

A new sign prominently appeared at the end of the car wash driveway, just before the customer exited the lot. It said, "If you are dissatisfied with your car wash, Loondance will happily rewash your car."

Workers were retrained on smiling, on courtesy, on

always saying "please" and "thank you." Canine riders received dog snacks. The car wash looked and felt more pleasant.

The car wash manager realized that all the original signs were actually advertising potential problems to customers. The signage was educating and alerting customers to look for damages. (There was one sign, for example, that exempted the car wash from responsibility for washing certain Ford models and certain SUVs. Naturally, every Ford customer went on red alert and assumed prior damages were caused that day.) The signage raised the consciousness of the customers to imaginable problems. And the signs raised awareness and red flags in an adversarial and challenging manner. The customers were going to war instead of going to a wash.

After the offensive signs were removed, the incidence of customer complaints plummeted from one or two a day to one or two a month.

The next time you are about to enter a store that assaults you with warning signs, stop and read the signs aloud. After reading the signs aloud, gauge your feeling for the store. Are you relaxed or tense? Are you positive or negative? Are you looking for purchases or problems?

Read these commonly found signs aloud.

```
NO SHOES
NO SHIRT
NO SERVICE
NO EATING
NO DRINKING
NO BATHROOMS
NO DOGS
NO STROLLERS
NO CHILDREN
NO CREDIT CARDS
```

Read these warm welcomes: "No cell phones! You would not have them on in a library. You will not have them on in here!" Or, "Puleeeze! *No* cell phones! This is *not* a phone booth." (Of course it is all right for this merchant if the company phone rings while people are shopping.) And this happy merchant not only chastises the customer upon entry but verbally spanks the customer on the way out with yet another version of the "No cell phones" sign. Contrast these signs with the discreetly placed, but not to be missed, reminder in a restaurant: "Cell phone ringing interferes with the preparation of your risotto." A bit nicer.

Marketing superstars turn negatives into positives. Superstars make things nice for the customer.

Marketing Superstar Instant Challenge #4 Answer

*A*fter consultation with the flower lady, and some scrounging, three poster board signs, tacked to tomato stakes, were consecutively placed by the roadside far enough apart to give drivers time to see them and stop. The three signs read:

Remember Her Tonight with Flowers!
Friday Night Is Flower Night!
Flower Power for Sale!

The power of suggestion is powerful marketing.

One additional sign was tacked to the rickety stand:

THE FLOWER LADY

Don't forget the brand name.

Phil Ochs would have been happy with the flower lady's new success.

• LVI •

Summary #1

HALLMARKS OF GREAT MARKETING COMPANIES

*T*he great marketing companies in this world have much in common. They continue to succeed, to grow in revenues and profits, to adapt to change and opportunity, and to inordinately influence society and their industries. They have the highest rates of return on assets and equity in their industries. Following are the hallmarks—the guiding principles—of the great marketing companies and of marketing superstars:

1. Achieving and keeping dominant market share in chosen significant niches is their priority. They fully understand that #1 or strong #2 market share in their niche is the fundamental common denominator of profitability.

2. Marketing superstars know that the #1 market share leaders almost always have the #1 profits, #1 awareness, strongest customer franchise and loyalty, and highest prices. This allows them to invest more in market research, more in R&D, and more in gaining share advantage over their competitors.

3. Superstars focus on market share as measured in units rather than sales dollars. They invest in market share utilizing some of today's profits for future market position.

4. Understanding the importance of market share leadership requires a sharp awareness of what business the company is really in—from a customer perspective—and what that translates to for positioning and niches. That's why great marketing companies know their niche customers and think about marketing strategy and then execute that strategy relentlessly.

5. Consequently, marketing superstars are constantly segmenting their markets into new niches, big and small, and executing their segment plans meticulously.

6. There is constant contact with customers. Superstars are open-minded. They suppress their ego. They observe customer behavior, changes in behavior, and emerging customer needs. They do lots of

listening. They hire objective outside professionals to give them honest answers.

7. The entire company is oriented toward marketing. *Everyone* in the company understands that marketing is the only renewing activity. Every employee values the customer.

8. In great companies, all top managers are customer-oriented, and they make sure all of the people they supervise are customer-oriented.

9. All top managers regularly make calls on customers.

10. The whole company serves the customer, not just the sales and marketing people, but production, human resources, financial, and research people as well.

11. Marketing superstars plan with absolutely clear, measurable specific goals; not just short-term, one-year goals, but those critical to implementing strategic vision.

12. Manufacturing and marketing people meet often, *once a week*, to discuss costs, forecasts, production, new products, and new processes.

13. R&D is rewarded for commercialized successes, not just technical ingenuity.

14. There is a constant review of competitive activity.

Superstars realize that competitors lurk and plot and want to steal every single customer.

15. Superstars invest more in the aggressive getting and keeping of customers than their competitors.

16. Application case histories and successful customer incidents are constantly communicated throughout the sales forces.

17. The sales function is considered part of the marketing mix and is overseen by a marketing manager. Great marketing companies understand that selling and distribution and advertising are not marketing, rather they are marketing functions.

18. Superstars do not make decisions based on the short-term shouts and pleas of the distributor or channel. Channels are not end-use customers. Channels are channels.

MARKETING SUPERSTARS . . .

19. See trade channels as partners, not customers.

20. Work relentlessly to create customer franchises.

21. Truly understand the importance of brand names and constantly work to keep the brand names known and untarnished.

22. Reduce uncertainty with meticulous homework and research. Superstars have a clear vision. They

know what business they are in. They know what their customers want. They give customers what they want.

23. Seek lots of opinions, especially from current and lapsed customers, from the suppliers, and from the people on the firing line.

24. Do not get surprised by changes in the market. Superstars usually influence the market.

25. Sell the dollarized value of *benefits,* not features, and not technology.

26. Create successful recipes by cooking together market data, intuitive marketing common sense, and contrarian ideas.

27. Price products to value, not to cost, and fearlessly sell that price.

28. Provide good, customized, and consistent sales training on how to sell dollarized value.

29. Preserve opportunity money to take advantage of unplanned opportunities.

30. Are maniacal about product quality; and quality is defined by their customers, not by manufacturing or quality assurance.

31. Believe that only the good, "Okay" customer is always right. Superstars work like crazy to find the right customer, to get lots of the right customers, and to keep all of those customers.

Summary #2

CHARACTERISTICS OF THE KILLER COMPETITOR COMPANIES

C ertain companies consistently lead, or dominate, their industries. They are feared by their competitors. Here are the reasons why they lead:

1. Marketing, in all forms, in detail, is the driving culture of the company.
2. Getting and keeping #1 or #2 market share in their selected niches is their most worthy marketing mission. They ruthlessly and relentlessly compete for market share. Making acquisitions is a growth strategy, to increase and defend market share.
3. They know precisely what business they are in, and use that knowledge for positioning their

products and company. And they stay in those businesses.

4. Procedures, processes, methods, no matter how sacrosanct or successful, are constantly under objective review. Every piece of the business is subject to rethinking, re-evaluation, and rerationalization. These companies constantly innovate.

5. They worship at the altar of product quality. Quality is defined by the customer. As the customer perceives the quality, so it is. There is no compromise on quality. Quality is a marketing, not a manufacturing, issue.

6. They are always making things better no matter how good they are. They do not leave well enough alone.

7. Management is expected to deal with the world the way it really is. Reality thinking is mandatory. Candor, honesty, questioning, homework, debate, and hardheaded clarity are the rules.

8. Change is understood to be a constant. These companies know that external environments are influenced by all kinds of factors, including competition. Change and the need to adapt are considered windows of opportunity. The company leaders do not fret; they think and act.

9. There is no illusion about the competitive environment. They recognize that competition is out to eat their lunch. They keep good competitive intelligence, particularly in areas of cost and innovation. Because they are innovators, their basic competitive strategy is to preempt competition and put them on the defensive. Because they want #1 market share they plan marketing strategy with care and execute that strategy perfectly.

10. Great athletic coaches and teams have a characteristic common to killer competitor companies: They recruit the best athletes, train them carefully, and put the best players on the field. They get good people in all levels and job functions.

11. Good companies prosper because of good people. However, census is considered a cancer. Hiring good people, but not a lot of people, is the guideline. This means not having a lot of layers in the company, especially between the CEO and the customer. Bureaucracy is the enemy.

12. If a person is not directly or indirectly responsible for getting and keeping customers, his or her job is not needed. In killer competitor companies, support services not relevant to the core business, such as cafeteria service and mailroom management, are farmed out to companies whose only

business, for example, is cafeteria services. It is better to buy services than to staff for them.

13. These companies understand it is better to own a market than a mill. Manufacturing takes direction from the marketplace.

14. The cutting of bureaucracy and layers and irrelevant factors is part of their culture. They eliminate parts, reduce meetings, speed analysis, cut memos, cut paperwork, cut steps, and free up time to make things simpler. To compete, the organization has to be quick, direct, and nimble.

15. They value strategy and execution, not endless planning and analysis. Their three most important words in strategy are "execution," "execution," "execution."

16. They look at markets globally and with a macro view. They consider global changes and scenarios. They play what-if war games: What might a competitor do? They put themselves in the shoes of the competitors, customers, and shareholders and look at their company through those eyes.

17. Everyone knows the company strategy, abides by the culture, helps to adapt and implement change no matter how wrenching, and knows how to get and keep customers.

EPILOGUE

*B*ecome a marketing superstar. Evaluate every marketing effort, every marketing dollar, every person in the organization according to the super marketer's anthem . . .

> ♪ It don't mean a thing. ♪
> If it don't go *ka-ching*!
> ♪ Doo-bop, doo-bop, doo-bop. ♪

Appendix: Dollarize Your Way to More Effective Marketing

A start-up company with a novel design for a high-capacity toner cartridge for laser printers faced a tricky marketing conundrum. The company, then named RTI, Inc., faced two groups of foes: the premium-priced, premium-quality industry giants; and the low-priced, marginal-quality "remanufacturers" (the thousands of shops that refilled and recycled used cartridges).

The challenge was to earn pricing in the league of the major players while not being sullied as another low quality remanufacturer. Dollarization helped show them the way.

The company leaned on its unique, patented advantage—more printed pages per cartridge—to create its own niche. They conducted testing with third-party laboratories that consistently showed that their product produced at least twice as many printed pages as the corresponding cartridges from the market leaders. They also had independent imaging experts analyze the quality of the printed images to verify that RTI produced images at least as good as the big players (this was an area where remanufacturers performed poorly).

To determine possible product pricing levels, RTI used a detailed dollarization analysis. That analysis follows.

THE SIX STEPS IN DOLLARIZATION AS USED BY RTI

1. Determine the Competition.

State the other options your customer will be considering. Options could include an existing methodology, a competitor, or an in-house customer approach.

Example: The competitor is a large supplier of original-equipment toner cartridges.

2. State Your Benefit.

State why your customer should do business with you.

Example: Our product produces more pages from the same amount of toner.

3. Quantify the Benefit.

Restate the benefit in numerical terms.

Example: "Produces more pages" means customers will need to buy two competitive cartridges to produce 15,000 pages, but only one of RTI's cartridges.

4. Dollarize the Benefit.

Calculate the dollar value of the benefit.

Example:

Extra Competitor Cartridges Required for 15,000 pgs.		Cost per Cartridge		Extra Competitive Purchase Costs
	×		=	
1	×	$150	=	$150

5. Express the Total Dollarized Benefit in "Per Unit" Terms.

Calculate the portion of the total economic benefit the customer realizes from each unit he purchases.

Example:

Extra Competitor Costs	÷	Number of RTI Cartridges	=	Savings per Cartridge
$150	÷	1	=	$150

6. *Demonstrate the True Total Cost of Your Competitor's Product.*

Show how the total economic benefit derived from each product reveals the true total cost (or true price) of your competitor's product.

Example:

Competitor's Price	+	Extra Cost	=	Competitor's True Price
$150	+	$150	=	$300

In other words, RTI demonstrated that a customer could buy a single cartridge from them for $150, or could spend $300 to buy two competitive cartridges, with both approaches yielding the same end result: 15,000 printed pages of acceptable quality. Further refinement of the dollarization analysis showed that the cartridge saved 0.5¢–1.0¢ per page in toner costs. RTI then looked at the other major consumable in laser printing: paper. It turns out that common copy paper often sells for approximately 0.5¢–1.0¢ per page. In other words, the toner cartridge savings paid for the paper upon which each page was printed.

RTI's entire marketing approach followed this understanding of its dollarized difference.

Company Positioning

The company needed to overcome any association with poor-quality remanufacturers. The company positioned itself as a new supplier of toner that produced better images than remanufacturers (and as good as any suppliers), and did so more economically than any supplier.

Corporate Name (Branding)

Based on the required quality image perception, the company name was changed from RTI (meaningless initials) to Clarity Imaging Technologies, with the nickname Clarity.

Product Positioning

The product was positioned as a "paper saver" rather than a "toner saver." This was contrary to the claims and positionings of the competition, and more appealing to the customers.

Branding

Based on the "paper saver" positioning, the product was branded Page Max®.

Segmentation

Clarity Imaging Technologies learned that some low-volume users were willing to accept the higher total cost of using the market leaders' branded cartridge. These users replaced their cartridges only once every year or two, and they were unwilling to give up the security of a big brand name for those savings. However, Clarity found that high-volume users, such as insurance companies and law firms, recognized that the Clarity cartridges could produce substantial savings. These companies also appreciated secondary benefits, such as reduced inventory of replacement cartridges, reduced handling, and other benefits that resulted from longer cartridge life. These segments became Clarity's prime target. No resources were wasted trying to appeal to other segments.

Advertising and Promotion

Based on the dollarization understanding and the product positioning, the advertising team produced the following tag line: "Page Max. It's like getting your paper for free."

Pricing

Page Max was priced to value, at a 5 percent premium to the market leaders' pricing. (The enormous value of the market leaders' brands, and their inherent pricing power, limited Clarity's ability to price the product at a greater premium.)

Selling

The sales teams charged with introducing this new product were trained to calculate the direct toner cartridge savings, to explore the other savings, and to educate the customer to what it was costing the customer to go without the savings. Sales worked with high-volume users to optimize the ordering and inventory of cartridges. Sales calculated the value of cutting in half all the handling costs involved . . . from replacing empty cartridges to packaging and returning old cartridges for recycling. Sales used a dollarization calculator to demonstrate to customers the true cost of Page Max versus other brands, and calculated the economic consequences of not adopting Page Max.